What professionals in the field are saying ...

"Maria Tadd has written an excellent resource guide for both senior adults and their families. As a geriatric care manager I find that I address almost every topic covered in this book with seniors and their families. Ms. Tadd's book covers a wide range of issues that, sooner or later, are a part of every family's discussions. When addressing these issues, "sooner" is always better than "later". Her material is a cogent guide to each topic. If seniors or family members take time to read only one book to guide their thoughts and actions, this is the book!"
— **J. William Crittenden, Geriatric Care Manager, Senior Care Management Associates, LLC, Chapel Hill, NC**

"Reading this book is like having a long conversation with a friend over coffee. You will learn in detail about the experience of long-distance caregiving including lessons learned, opinions offered, and suggestions made. This thought-provoking book will prepare you to help an elder maintain a positive lifestyle in her home. The book is very comprehensive and covers most anything you might need to know. Be sure to look through the Appendix section, where the questionnaires will help you navigate and choose correctly the assistance your elder needs."
— **Jeanne Martin, MSW, MTS, Ed.D., Geriatric Social Worker and Consultant, Boston, MA**

"Ms. Tadd has adroitly deflected indignation suffered through her mother's final days, transforming the energy eloquently to inform others facing similar challenges in caring for an aging parent. She offers vital, timely, and life-affirming suggestions, while alerting caregivers to avoid the pitfalls she experienced. With its holistic perspective, weaving tai chi and state-of-the-art technology, this will prove to be an indispensable guide for adult children of aging parents and for professional care providers as well."
— **Paula Craige, PT, Geriatric Care Manager, Chapel Hill, NC**

"What a valuable book for anyone facing or currently providing care for a loved one! I can't imagine a more complete compendium of resources and of pitfalls to avoid. Filled with checklists and other guides, this book provides practical help with the important decisions that must be made. Readers will benefit from the lessons personally learned by the author and from her extensive research throughout, and after, her caregiving experiences.

If you want to be prepared for, or need help with, caring for your aging parent, spouse, or other loved one, this is the book to read and use."

— **Anna Niemtiz, Ph.D., Chapel Hill, NC**

Tadd, Maria
    Happiness Is Growing Old at Home/ by Maria Tadd
       p.   cm.
    Includes index.
    ISBN 978-0-9823081-0-3
    1. Aging parents—maintaining independence. 2. Cost-effective models of care. 3. High-tech devices help seniors age in place. 4. Screening tools for providers and facilities.

Cover design by Shannon Dancy. Book layout by Karen Newton.

Library of Congress Control Number: 2008911549

Happiness Is Growing Old at Home

Discover New Ways to Help Your Aging Parent Remain Independent

Maria Tadd

Terrapin Press

Chapel Hill, North Carolina

Acknowledgements

First, I want to thank my mother, Maria A. Gilgut, who often offered me encouragement during my later adult years and was a champion of my many ideas and inventions. The challenges she faced as a 95-year-old widow living alone in her house were the inspiration for my writing this book. While coordinating her care, I witnessed firsthand the difficulties confronting caregivers in identifying and securing competent, compassionate support services. I quickly discovered that acquiring services is not that simple, and that the quality of care runs the gamut. As I joined my mother on her odyssey, I learned what worked and what didn't.

Since her death, I have done a great deal of research and have discovered that the field of geriatrics is burgeoning with innovations. A global initiative is underway to create new devices and new paradigms that can help elders age in place. The novelty and creativity of these new inventions and models are nothing short of mind-boggling. With a naissance of new products, it is difficult to keep abreast of what is new, and most people are unaware of what is available.

Writing this book has been a long process. I started writing it while my mother was alive, and she actually read parts of it before she passed away. It was my intention to finish it within a few months. But as I worked on it, it actually took on a life of its own and became a very different book from the one I had started. Instead of simply sharing what I learned while trying to navigate the health care system, it morphed into a book that is now rich with the latest information on how to help seniors live independently longer.

Because I did not have the luxury of simply writing, I had to carve out blocks of time. I found that at times I was very motivated and driven — then there were those periods during which I just couldn't work on it. This past fall, nearly two years past my self-imposed deadline, I was so close and yet so far. While having brunch one day, a friend suggested that she prod me a bit — so every day for a week I received an e-mail: "Have you hugged your book today?" Thank you, Christine Hill! It was just what I needed.

I would like to thank my good friends, Richard Morrison and Paul Gallagher, for their ongoing support and advice. They were always available during this entire process, and they tirelessly responded to my numerous e-mails regarding title selection, press names, photos, and content, and basically helped me each step of the way. My mother thought of them as her sons, in part, because they are like brothers to me. Thank you, dear "bros."

I would also like to thank all of my reviewers: Paula Craig, J. William Crittenden, Carol De Poix, Jeanne Martin, Anna Niemitz, and Cheryl Tarish. Special thanks go to Cheryl for her very thoughtful and thorough comments and review and to Anna for her helpful critique and suggestions. You both gave me great feedback.

And finally, I would like to thank Jennie Ratcliffe for her impeccable editing, Karen Newton for doing a wonderful job laying out the text, and my designer, Shannon Dancy, for producing a beautiful cover that captures the spirit of growing old. The colored pencil drawings were made by her mother, E. A. Newton, in her later years.

I hope you find that "Happiness Is Growing Old at Home" is an enjoyable read as well as an invaluable resource that will help you and your parent share this once-in-a-lifetime journey.

Dedication

In loving memory of my mother, Maria A. Gilgut
a.k.a. Aurelia Maria Bochnar
May 28, 1911 - October 22, 2006

Contents

Chapter 3
Managing My Mother's Care: Practical Tips

Chapter 4
What I Learned: Specific Suggestions

Chapter 5
Guidelines and Questions to Ask Home Health
Care Agencies, Rehab Facilities, and Hospice

Introduction

Facts to ponder:

- *Seniors fear going into a nursing home and losing their independence more than death.*[1]
- *Eight-two percent of baby boomers fear their parents will be mistreated in a nursing home, and 89% fear their parents will be sad.*[1]
- *In 2008, a study conducted by the U.S. Department of Health and Human Services found that 94% of nursing homes (~16,000) in the United States were in violation of federal health and safety standards.*

Home Sweet Home

How many times have we heard "There's no place like home," or "Home is where the heart is"? After all, nothing is more nurturing than being in an environment that is familiar — one that feels a bit like a pair of well-worn slippers.

The familiar incorporates all aspects of life, not just the walls that house so many memories. It includes the cultivation of long-lasting friendships developed over time; caring

1

neighbors who provide a sense of security and well-being and who check in from time to time or bring freshly picked tomatoes from their garden; and a trusted team of physicians and other health care providers. It includes the threadbare carpet, the dingy walls that cry out for a new coat of paint, the chipped countertop, the old, over-stuffed, leather recliner, and memories of days gone by — the joys, the laughter, the good times, and the not-so-good times. It is basically the context and content of one's life.

As our parents age in place, their surroundings also change with the passage of time. The landscape matures, neighbors get older, and children eventually leave the nest. Little pines planted when the house was built are now tall and majestic and provide privacy and shade. Flowering shrubs that once dotted the landscape now dwarf their former selves and predictably bloom year after year, gracing the yard with a richly colored palette. And after years of meticulous maintenance, the lush, green lawn beckons to caress the soles of those who tread upon it. This, too, becomes part of what is familiar.

Some neighbors come and go, but if your parent is fortunate, many have remained. How lovely it is to see a friendly face, have a neighborly chat, or pet the old dog next door during afternoon strolls. Or walk through rooms filled with keepsakes held dear. How liberating it is to wake up according to one's own biological clock, to eat breakfast mid-morning, to go outside and listen to the songbirds, feel the warmth of the sun and be one with nature — to be among all those little treasures in life that feed the soul. To give up one's life as one has lived it for decades can be a truly frightening prospect.

And so it is no surprise that our elders want to remain in their homes where they feel safe, comfortable, and, above all, happy. Study after study confirms that they want to age in place. When asked, up to 90% of American elders have said they want to die at home. But the harsh reality is that 80% die in nursing homes and hospitals.[2] Furthermore, a recent survey of baby boomers found that 80% want to remain in their homes and in their neighborhoods.[3] Given the size of our aging population, for these wishes to be realized we need to look at a wide variety of available resources, including alternative nontraditional, residential models and high-tech devices. We must also continue to design and develop innovative solutions that will allow our elders and baby boomers to age in place.

Even before our parents start to decline physically or mentally or become ill, the thought of moving seems overwhelming. And although many elders do not realize the potential for isolation after they have become widowed, in the end, isolation still seems preferable to being uprooted and having to start over again, to make new friends, find new doctors, find a new hair stylist, and to adjust to new surroundings.

Like so many seniors, my mother and stepfather also feared going into a nursing home. Consequently, they made a pact that regardless of their condition they would not put the other in one. And even when my stepfather became quite ill from cancer, with the help of health care aides and hospice he remained at home until he passed away in 2000. I too promised my mother that I would never put her in a nursing home and — once again, with the help of health care aides, hospice, and her absolutely wonderful neighbors and friends — my mother's wish was granted.

Some might say that nursing homes have been given a bad rap. I'll let you be the judge. Go to a few facilities and apply the litmus test yourself. While you are there, look around and imagine what it would be like to "live" there.

Just for a moment put yourself in your parent's shoes. Would you want to spend your final months or days in a nursing home, hospital or — even worse — an Intensive Care Unit (ICU)? Is this where you would want to be as your life draws to a close?

Regardless of one's religious beliefs, we probably can all agree that dying in a nurturing, loving environment, surrounded by family and friends, is what we would wish for ourselves and for our loved ones. One cannot die peacefully in an environment that is sterile, dispassionate, noisy, and the antithesis of being at home. Alarms go off during all hours of the night and day, staff often perform painful and humiliating procedures, and fluorescent light fills the space that welcomes the dark.

If your parent is in the hospital or even in an ICU, if you can possibly bring her home, do it. It is one of the final and greatest gifts you can give her.

After my 95-year-old mother broke her pelvis, and after a 10-day hospital stay failed to stabilize her, we were told to bring her home to die. She actually made a miraculous recovery while at home and went into rehab, but shortly thereafter she began her decline. Over the years, I had promised her that I would make sure that she would be able to die at home, and on October 22, 2006, she passed away in her own bed with dignity and grace. And even though there was a rough patch during the 24-hour period immediately prior to her slipping into a deep sleep, in the end she was comfortable. When she died, a serenity and sacredness permeated her room.

During the time my mother was hospitalized for her broken pelvis, I visited quite a few nursing homes and rehab facilities and it became painfully obvious why even a short stay can be remarkably dehumanizing and depressing. The regimentation, the lack of choice, and the institutional environment cannot promote healing or well-being. My mother's 7-week rehab stay in a relatively upscale nursing home was fraught with problems, mostly due to the ubiquitous staff shortages that plague every nursing home in America. However, this is no excuse, as some of the problems she encountered were potentially life-threatening.

As we watch our parents age and perhaps begin to show signs of frailty, we need to have an honest discussion with them as to where they want to live out their days as well as their viable options in terms of finances, support services, and the possibility of other residential models. Most will say they want to age at home and that they do not want to move into a retirement community, assisted living, or a nursing home. If your parents are like my mother, then you too may have heard, *"I don't want to be around other old peo-*

ple." However, sooner or later, because of changes in either their physical and/or mental status, they will need assistance. And when that time comes, often unexpectedly, the more information you have at your disposal, the better equipped you will be to hire the services that will be right for your loved one.

If you don't do your homework before a crisis occurs, you will find that there are not enough hours in a day to make all the calls, screen the various agencies, and try to put all of the many pieces together that will enable your parent to stay at home or be able to return home after a hospital or rehab stay.

I therefore strongly encourage you to do your research before your parent is actually in need of assistance. With no time constraints, you will be able to contact various agencies that can assist you with identifying services your parent may need. With their help, you will be able to take an inventory of what is available in your area. When you are not stressed out and pressed to find services, you can query agencies in a more relaxed way.

Having the luxury of time could spare you from making a decision you might regret later on. Be sure to check references and see what previous clients liked or disliked about particular agencies. In addition, get some recommendations about rehab facilities and, if necessary, nursing homes. If you have time to scope these out before you need them, you will be way ahead of the game.

I pride myself on being a problem solver and a one-person think tank who plans for the unexpected and has a backup plan for everything. But in spite of making what appeared to be a comprehensive "what if" list with a solution for every conceivable problem, there were always surprises. After all, life is dynamic and things are constantly changing.

The overwhelming desire to age in place presents us with a unique opportunity to find creative ways to make this happen. People around the world are working on innovative devices and new paradigms to address the needs of the elderly. Every month new technologies are unveiled, and even more are in the pipeline. Communities are also working together to develop more options.

In addition to aging in place, other residential alternatives are now available:

- Small group homes where three or four residents share the cost of in-home care
- The Beacon Hill Village model, where elders and other members of the community provide assistance to elders living at home
- Green Houses, with 6–10 individuals who require skilled nursing
- Granny flats, which are temporary housing units that can be placed on the property of a relative or friend.

All of these options, plus new high-tech devices and technologies, will be covered in this book. Because new devices and alternatives continue to enter the market at a rapid pace, you can go to http://www.agingathome.info to find the latest updates.

Assisting our aging population to remain in their homes reduces the economic burden placed on our society and government. So it is incumbent on all of us to tap into our creative juices and work collectively to solve this problem.

This book is designed to help you navigate the system, learn about options, and steer you away from some of the hazards I encountered. You will find a treasure-trove of ideas, practical solutions, and problem-solving tips that will be invaluable if you are trying to manage your elderly parent's care at home either locally or from a distance. I hope my experiences, trials, tribulations, and suggestions will prepare you for the unexpected and help you resolve issues in a timely manner. With any luck, my story and the many lessons you can glean from my experiences will provide you with what you need to make the system work for you and your loved one. If I have done my job well, this book should help you avoid the pitfalls that caused me grief, time, and money.

How to Get the Most Out of This Book

"An ounce of prevention is worth a pound of cure."
– Ben Franklin

This book is divided into six sections:

Chapter 1 is an overview of how to assess your parent's home to make it safer; how to evaluate her physical and emotional needs; how to introduce in-home care; how to broach difficult subjects; and what types of documents should be in place.

Chapter 2 provides a holistic approach to creating a care plan. It includes the importance of living a healthy lifestyle; the latest high-tech devices and gadgets that can help seniors live independently longer and give caregivers peace of mind; some of the options within in-home care and what other supportive services are in your area; new residential alternatives; and how to pay for their care.

Chapter 3 is my story about dealing with the health care system, home health care aides and hospice, and trying to manage my mother's care from afar. It is full of practical tips that are both in the main text and call-out boxes. If you are short on time, just read the call-out boxes, and you will find helpful hints without much time or effort.

Chapter 4 offers concrete suggestions as to how you can make in-home health care work for you even if you are not around to oversee the caregivers.

Chapter 5 is a list of questions that I wish I had known to ask when putting together my mother's care plan.

And finally, the last section contains the **Appendices**, with sample schedules and questionnaires, flow charts, a list of annotated Web sites grouped by topics, and recommended reading. A list of references and trademarks used in the book can also be found in this section.

The in-home health care industry is a big business and offers a range of services with an even wider range of fees. Even when you think you are on top of the latest offerings, there may be new initiatives that you are unaware of. For example, currently there is a movement to change the parameters of residential hospice care. Traditionally, residential hospice has been available to people whose life expectancy was 6 months or less and who were willing to forego further treatment. As a result, many people end up in residential hospice for a relatively short time. Now this very caring, humane service may be available for a longer period of time, which will ultimately help our loved ones and also reduce some of the burden faced by family members. Some states are now also allowing people to receive treatment such as chemotherapy or radiation while in residential or in-home hospice, so you need to stay on top of this ever-changing industry.

Residential hospices are truly wonderful, and if for some reason a parent cannot die at home, they are the next best thing.

During my mother's rehab and illness, I spent four months learning what works, what doesn't, and what you can do to make it work for you. It is imperative that you do your homework or hire someone to do it for you. And remember, "Buyer beware"!

PLEASE Note: The content of this book applies to all aging parents, but in an attempt to avoid the clumsiness of "his or her" and "he and she," I have elected to use "her" and "she" with the non-gender-specific "parent."

> DISCLAIMER: Information on herbs, supplements, vitamins, medicines, and exercise provided in this book is intended for educational purposes ONLY and is NOT intended to suggest or recommend treatment. Before your parent adds vitamins or herbs to her diet or tries a new exercise program, she should consult her physician first. Note: This disclaimer applies to a parent of either gender.

CHAPTER 1

*An Overview of Issues and Options
to Help Your Parent
Live Independently Longer*

*"We have succeeded in helping people live longer.
Now we have to help them live better."*
— Anonymous

Study after study clearly suggests that seniors will be happier if they are able to age in the comfort of their own home. However, wanting to remain at home and being able to remain at home are two different stories. Many seniors fear that they will be forced to move because of the possibility of a decline in their physical or mental status or because they will no longer be able to drive. For some, their children may tell them that it is not safe for them to live alone and may encourage, or insist, that their parent move into assisted living or a nursing home.

Before anyone makes any decisions about relocation, which can be quite traumatic for your parent, read this book.

Learn about all of the options available today. From finding ways to make homes structurally safer and more senior-friendly, to learning about the latest high-tech devices, to tapping into community resources (some of which might surprise you), or hiring in-home care, you can create a mix of available options that may provide your loved one with just what she needs. Your parent will be allowed to age with compassion and grace at home and everyone will have peace of mind.

Let's compare costs

In addition to honoring the wishes of our parent, we know that keeping our parent in her home reduces the economic burden for both families and society at large. Assisted living and nursing homes are extremely expensive, and the latter often cause tremendous emotional suffering for our parent as well as for ourselves.

Be creative. With a broad range of options from which to choose, you can mix and match various services, monitoring systems, and high-tech devices, and create innovative alternative models of care that will save you money. The following cost comparisons are based on 2007 data and reflect regional differences:

- **Assisted living:** $1,963-$5,031 per month and a yearly national average of around **$36,000**.
- **Nursing home:** $128-$300 per day or an annual cost of $46,720-$109,500; the national average is

between **$67,000 and $78,000** per year. The rehab unit in the nursing home where my mother stayed cost $270 a day or $98,550 a year (in 2006). Medicare generally covers the first 100 days of rehab. If you have supplemental insurance, it may cover 80% of the costs after the initial 100 days. Of course, this coverage varies among providers. If your parent has long-term care insurance, some of these costs might be covered, depending on their policy.

- **An example of an innovative cost-effective model of care:**
    - Install a passive monitoring system (see Chapter 2 for a description of this "smart" system). Typically, these systems cost around $200-$1,000 for installation and activation plus a $40-$90 monthly fee.
    - Install MedSignals®, an electronic pillbox that enhances and monitors compliance. Currently the initial setup fee is $49 and there is a $29/month fee with a 12-month contract.
    - Hire an in-home health care aide who can help with shopping, cleaning, laundry, running errands, picking up prescriptions, transportation, etc. If your parent needs only minimal assistance, try starting out with just 6 hours a week. The national hourly rate for a certified nursing assistant (CNA) is $19. Contrast the cost of this model with either a nursing home or

assisted living and the savings are huge. This particular model of care will cost around **$7,356** plus the initial one-time expense of $249-$1,049 for installations of the passive monitoring system and electronic pillbox. Your parent will be able to remain in her home where she will be safe and happy and you won't have to worry about her.

Cost-$aving Tips

	National Average*	Yearly Costs
Nursing home	$67,000-$78,000/ year*	$46,720-$109,500/ year ($128-$300/day)
Assisted living	$36,000/year*	$23,556-$60,375/year ($1,963-$5,031/ month)
Innovative model of care		
CNA, 6 hr/week	$19/hr.*	$19/hr × 6 hours × 52 weeks = $5,928
Passive monitoring	$200-$1,000 for installation $40-$90/month	$90 × 12 months = $1,080
MedSignals electronic pillbox	$49 installation and $29/month	$29 × 12 months = $348 **Total: $7,356/year** (plus one-time installation fees)
Annual cost savings based on mean		
Innovative model vs. Nursing home **$65,100**		
Innovative model vs. Assisted living **$28,644**		

Even if your parent needs more in-home care than presented in the model above, you will still save money by allowing her to live in the comfort of her home.

While researching this book, I read a story about a businessman, an only child and the father of six, and his elderly mother, who was widowed, blind, and diabetic. He took her to dialysis three days a week and a health care aide picked her up and helped with dinner and other chores. With just three hours a day of in-home care, his mother was able to live at home until three days before she passed away.

 Using the national average of $19/hour for a CNA, her care for one year would have cost $20,748, about $16,000 less than assisted living and $52,000 less than a nursing home.

The sad reality is that for some parents, a nursing home may be the only option. As much as you and your parent would like it to be otherwise, in some cases safety might have to trump happiness. If your parent uses a walker and needs help with activities of daily life (ADLs) and no longer has the strength to get out of bed, or perhaps has already had a couple of falls, then depending on finances, your choices may be slim. And even though nursing homes are frightfully expensive, round-the-clock in-home care is even more expensive. If you find that this is your situation, please evaluate potential facilities by using the questionnaire in Appendix A on assessing rehab facilities and by using the new federal 5-star rating system which is now available at http://www.Medicare.gov/NHCompare. Another helpful resource is http://www.MemberoftheFamily.net, which provides free reports based on government findings of 16,000 nursing homes. This site includes a National Watch List that lists nursing homes cited for numerous violations or those that have had numerous, substantiated complaints.

 If your parent owns her own home and needs greater liquidity, she could explore the possibility of getting a reverse mortgage. The Web site http://www.reversemortgage.org/ provides a calculator that will help you determine how much your parent qualifies for, and who knows, it may be enough for in-home care. Twenty-four hour live-in care costs much less than having an agency provide CNAs around the clock. Be creative. There may be someone from her church who needs a job and would like to help out, or a nursing student who may welcome free room and board plus a stipend in exchange for helping your parent.

Another factor that should be considered if you decide that your only option for your parent is either assisted living or a nursing home is the impact of "relocation stress syndrome," also called "transfer trauma." This is a formal diagnosis that is defined as physiologic and/or psychosocial disturbances due to being transferred from one environment to another. For some, the symptoms of relocation stress cause changes in one's health, personality, or disposition. If your parent is pre-disposed to depression, these symptoms could be exacerbated. For others, the changes are subtle. Preparing your loved one before moving her into a residential facility may minimize the negative effects. If the transfer occurs abruptly, the consequences can be severe, resulting in grave illness or even death. And individuals who are cognitively impaired (with Alzheimer's or dementia) may experience greater difficulty in adjusting to a new environment.

When I placed my mother in rehab, she was quite vehemently opposed to going. Once there, she had a hard time adjusting. She was emotionally distressed and repeatedly asked that I take her back home. I had never seen her so agitated. I wish I had known more about relocation stress; perhaps I could have better managed her transfer. On the positive side, being in rehab made it possible for her to walk again.

The increasing costs of care with each passing year, coupled with the desire to do what is best for maintaining the well-being of our seniors, make it incumbent upon us as a society to find ways to facilitate keeping our parents at home, in an environment that is nurturing and safe. After all, this is where they want to be. With a bit of commitment, research, and ingenuity it can be done. The issues at hand include:

- Assessing what changes need to be made to the home environment to make it safer and more elder-friendly

- What kinds of lifestyle changes our parent can make to provide her with a better quality of life
- Which organizations or private agencies can provide the necessary services to allow them to age in place: church groups, the Visiting Nurses Association (VNA), Meals On Wheels, student interns, high-school students, and in-home care
- The use of innovative high-tech devices

These are all part of the mix that can lead to greater independence. Baby boomers should pay close attention to the unfolding of these options, as they may be facing similar dilemmas and choices in the not-too-distant future. Like their parents, baby boomers have voiced their desire to age in place as well. Finding solutions for our parents will create a road map for aging baby boomers and for generations to come.

The first steps to helping your parent age at home

Step 1 — Get a home assessment to make sure her home is safe.

As your parent ages, her needs may change with respect to many physical aspects of her house, as certain items may now be potential hazards. There are two types of home assessments to help you determine what modifications should be made. One is typically done by an occupational therapist (OT) who checks for dangers in the house such as throw rugs or carpeting that might cause elders to trip, whether the bath tub is safe or if grab bars are needed, if the person can safely use doorknobs or if these need to be replaced with door levers, if the stove top is safe, if the refrigerator needs to be replaced with one with a bottom freezer, if the lighting is adequate, or if any furniture needs to be rearranged.

A second type of assessment can be made by a certified aging-in-place specialist designated by the National Association of Home Builders. These specialists are rather new to the market and may also cover some of the same areas addressed by the OT. In addition to making suggestions about lighting and replacing doorknobs, they also look at ways to remodel a home so that it is more elder-friendly. They may suggest that a bathroom and/or bedroom be installed on the first floor or that doorways be widened to accommodate a wheelchair. Their assessment includes simple modifications such as improving the lighting in the stairwell or replacing toilets with ones that are elevated, installing grab bars in the bathrooms, replacing hard-to-enter bathtubs with a walk-in shower, installing a shower seat, raising outlets and lowering light switches, elevating front-loading washers and dryers, etc. Some of the major renovations can be costly, but fortunately there are many aging-in-place projects that are trying to identify economical ways to make these improvements, especially in kitchens and bathrooms, so that elders can safely remain in their homes.

If your parent's home has stairs and she is showing signs of becoming unsteady or disabled, don't despair. There is a stair-climbing wheelchair now available. It is not covered by most insurance carriers, as they view it as a convenience device, but if you have the financial resources, this could be an option for you. And keep checking — someday, Medicare or supplemental insurance may pay for it.

Step 2 — Make sure your parent has up-to-date medical exams, both mental and physical.

As people age, changes occur within the brain that lead to differences in thinking and behavior. Differentiating what is normal aging from what might be the beginning of abnormal disease can be challenging. Sometimes changes in how someone acts socially or how she performs tasks can raise concerns. In addition to the diagnosis of dementia and Alzheimer's disease, there is another diagnosis called "cognitive impairment but not dementia" (CIND), which is a state somewhere between normal aging and dementia. And then add to the mix that changes in cognition could also be due to depression. Fortunately, physicians have a variety of cognitive assessment tools at their disposal to skillfully determine if your parent is experiencing normal aging or is manifesting the early signs of a cognitive disorder.

The most commonly used test to evaluate cognitive decline is the Mini Mental State Examination (MMSE) which takes about 8-10 minutes. It includes 30 questions and samples various functions including arithmetic, memory, and orientation. Most doctors who treat the elderly should be able to administer this type of screening test.

Even if your parent is mentally sharp, you may begin to notice some physical changes. She may tire more easily, she may not be as strong as she used to be, she may be experiencing balance issues, or her appetite may not be as good as it once was. Having an extensive physical exam may help determine the causes of these changes. It could be as simple as a new medication that is causing fatigue or making her feel unsteady on her feet.

Once you have gathered all of the up-to-date assessments from your parent's physicians, social worker, neurologist, and/or psychiatrist/psychologist, everyone will be on the same page, and you can have a candid discussion with your parent and your siblings so you can put a plan into place. After you determine what your parent needs, you can start to identify the best resources to help her age in place. Initially your parent may require a minimal amount of support such as Meals On Wheels, or perhaps an arrangement could be made with someone from her church or with a neighbor who would be willing to bring dinner a few nights a week.

Step 3 — Monitor your parent's status regularly.

There are some simple ways to assess if your parent is beginning to lose her cognitive ability. You can see if she is still able to explain things in detail or if she seems confused when trying to retell a story. Or you might notice that she gets frustrated or agitated easily. If you are concerned about her cognitive function, mention your concerns the next time she has a doctor's appointment. The doctor may perform a cognitive assessment like the MMSE described above or may request other tests such as an MRI.

Observe how she walks. Does she seem less steady on her feet? Does she have trouble getting up from a chair? Is it more difficult to get up from the sofa than from a wooden chair with arms? Is she beginning to shuffle? Has her appetite changed?

Make sure that the proper bars have been installed in bathrooms and that all stairs have railings on both sides that run the length of the stairs. Remove all throw rugs and mats and check to see if there are any loose bits of carpet. Make sure that stairs are properly covered to provide the greatest amount of traction. Remove any electric cords that run across a room or in front of a chair. If an electric space heater is used, position it so that it does not pose a tripping hazard and is not placed too close to flammable material. If your parent needs a cane or a walker to help with balance, make sure that a physical therapist takes the proper measurements so that the cane or walker is the right height. A cane that is too short can add to poor balance.

Helpful advice on how to prevent falls

According to the Centers for Disease Control and Prevention (CDC), falls are the leading cause of injury deaths in people 65 years of age and older. The National Osteoporosis Foundation estimates that 300,000 people suffer hip fractures each year, which are often caused by falls. An average of 24% of patients with hip fractures who are 50 years old or older die within a year of the fracture. Many patients who survive end up being disabled for the rest of their lives.[4]

Medications that have side effects such as drowsiness or disorientation can increase the risk of falling. And prescription medications are not the only culprits. It is important to pay close attention to over-the-counter cold and flu medications, as they can often increase drowsiness.

Staying active is one of the best ways to maintain muscle integrity and balance. Some exercises have proven to be more beneficial in reducing the incidence of falls than others. A new study suggests that yoga might reduce falls, and tai chi and Pilates can improve balance. Although yoga can be helpful for balance while standing, tai chi and Pilates are more effective at improving control and coordination while walking.[5] By strengthening the hip and leg joints and the body's core — the abdominal and back muscles — seniors can reduce their risk of falling.

Another important measure that should be taken to minimize the risk of falling is to make sure that stairs are well-lit and that nightlights are placed in strategic areas. Poor vision can also increase the risk of falling, so make sure your parent's eyes are checked annually.

For more information about learning how to prevent falls, visit http://newoldage.blogs.nytimes.com. Jane Gross lists links to a video called "The Good News on Fall Prevention," a list of medications that can increase the risk of falls, and much more. Also, the CDC's Web site (http://www.cdc.gov) has a great deal of information on how to prevent falls.

Step 4 — Introducing assistance — old versus new models of care.

As your parent becomes more frail either physically and/or mentally, she may need help with activities of daily living, and she may need to be reminded to take her medications or to attend doctor's appointments, or she may need someone to help her with meal preparation and cleanup.

When is it time to introduce assistance? Be clear as to what type of assistance she needs, given the state of her physical and mental health.

Some questions that may help you decide the kind of assistance your parent needs:

- Does she need help with meals?
- Can she get by with microwavable frozen dinners?
- Does she need assistance with washing dishes and cleaning up?
- Does she need to be reminded when to take her medications?
- Is she eating and drinking enough and with adequate frequency?
- Does she need to be reminded to bathe or toilet herself?
- Is she getting to doctors' appointments?
- Is she still able to go grocery shopping?
- Is she still going to church?
- Can she still do the laundry?
- Does she have companionship?
- Does she seek companionship?
- Is she engaged in meaningful activities?
- Does she still read the morning paper?
- Does she still root for her favorite teams?
- Does she chat like she used to, or has she become withdrawn?

Tried and true versus new high-tech devices

Depending on your answers to the questions above, you can research what is available in her area and determine which resources will be most easily accepted by your parent. She may be happy with mainstays such as Meals On Wheels or in-home care. Or she may not want a stranger in her house but would be amenable to having an electronic pillbox that would cue her to take her meds.

Simple changes may be less unsettling. Perhaps she would be willing to wear a new high-tech shirt which detects falls. (Currently one is available in the U.S. although it is not being marketed to seniors yet. The other was developed in Singapore and has not yet made it to our shores.) When the person falls, an alarm goes off and sends a signal to a mobile phone or a computer alerting relatives or friends. This can be life-saving. Or your parent may be willing to have a passive monitoring system installed that keeps you informed as to how she is faring and can also notify caregivers if there has been a change in routine, perhaps indicating a fall or other serious event.

Unlike the more typical Lifeline® model, consisting of a panic button that is worn around the neck or wrist, passive monitoring systems provide a whole new level of assistance which goes beyond emergency response buttons. (For more information, see pages 57-59.)

Currently there is little federal health care reimbursement for such devices. As the baby boomers age and require more and more assistance, these kinds of monitoring devices will become more prolific because they will help folks live independently longer as well as being a partial answer to the shortage of in-home care providers.

See Chapter 2 for more information about high-tech devices.

Step 5 — How to talk about driving.

One of the hardest decisions for an aging parent to make is to give up driving, as it is a symbol of independence. My stepfather drove until he was 90, the year that he died. Although he never had an accident, as a passenger I can attest to the fact that it often was a white-knuckle driving experience. For some reason, he tended to gun the engine as he turned on to a road when there was a car within sight to his left. Clearly his guardian angel was quite busy!

My mother, who was widowed at 88, drove until she was 92 and then decided on her own that she no longer felt safe behind the wheel. At first she stopped driving at night and then gave it up altogether. She no longer had the confidence in herself, worried about her reflexes, and did not want to pose a danger to herself and others. **In most states, the only requirement older seniors need to meet to renew a driver's license is to pass the eye exam, something my mother was able to do even when she was in her 90s.**

Here is a checklist that may help you determine if your parent is driving safely:

- Does she merge or change lanes without looking?

- Does she have trouble staying in the lane?
- Have you noticed her driving down a one-way street the wrong way?
- Has she driven down the wrong side of the street?
- Does she turn from the wrong lane?
- Does she gun the engine at inappropriate times?
- Does she brake at inappropriate times?
- Does she have a tendency to stop at a green light or in the middle of an intersection?
- Does she sometimes mistake the gas pedal for the brake pedal?
- Does she get lost in familiar places?
- Are traffic signs and signals confusing?
- Does she run stop signs or red lights without realizing it?
- Does she have close calls, i.e., come close to hitting cars, people or objects without realizing it?
- Does she drive much slower than the speed limit?

For more information on how to talk with your loved one about driving, go to: http://web.mit.edu/agelab/projects_driving.shtml.

Recognizing that driving is the gateway to independence, MIT's AgeLab is studying a myriad of interrelated factors that determine if one is fit to be behind the wheel. By taking an integrative approach that includes cognitive psychology, gerontology, medicine, engineering and planning, the Age-Lab is conducting research that examines the many factors that contribute to one's ability to drive safely. They are also researching how health and medicine affect one's ability to drive. One of their primary focuses is on understanding how older adults perceive their own driving ability and/or decide that it is time to stop driving, and the role of families in the driving decision. They also are working collaboratively with many car manufacturers in designing new technologies that will promote safe lifelong driving. Stay tuned.

Step 6 — Being organized can minimize a lot of potential stress.

Organize important documents while your parent is still healthy.

My stepfather was quite organized and he actually had a filing system in place. But after he passed away, any semblance of organization simply disappeared. So if your parent is like my mother, you can save yourself a lot of headaches and time if you put together a system that will work for you. I suggest either buying a three-ring binder with pockets, colored plastic envelopes that you can label or a simple expandable file.

Even if your parent is still able to pay her bills, talk with her financial advisor, and keep up with changes to her estate plan, you will still want to have copies of all her important documents just in case your parent experiences a catastrophic event such as a stroke, heart attack, or accident of some kind. You do not want to have to go searching for these documents during a crisis.

Documents that should be included are:

- <u>Legal documents</u>: will and trust, durable power of attorney, health care power of attorney, living will, advance health care directive, car registration (make sure the inspection sticker is up to date), car insurance policy, homeowner's insurance policy, car title, copy of the deed to the house, etc.

- <u>Insurance/medical information</u>: copies of contacts and ID numbers, copies of her social security card, Medicare card and other supplemental or long-term care insurance cards, names and phone numbers of all physicians, and list of medications. Create a matrix or a log that documents all doctors' visits, outcomes, medications, etc.

- <u>Support services</u>: Names, phone numbers and brochures of home health care agencies, the senior center, Meals On Wheels, Council on Aging, the VNA, and the local hospital.

- Create a cheat sheet with all the important names and numbers so that you will have everything you need at your fingertips. (See Appendix B, Information Management Sheet.)

Do yourself a favor — keep important numbers with you at all times. Key important names and phone numbers into your cell phone. You won't believe how handy this can be, plus it provides a backup for your paper list.

Step 7 — Consider hiring a geriatric care manager if you find that you need assistance in identifying resources or that you are simply stretched to the limit.

If your parent lives in a city or town with which you are unfamiliar, or even if you live nearby but simply do not know where to start in terms of looking for services, a geriatric care manager will be of immense help.

Many of us think we can do it all, but we find ourselves in what is called the Sandwich Generation, a term that has been around for decades. It refers to people who have to care for their own families, meeting the needs of their children, while caring for a parent. Today the demands are even greater as people are working more and have less free time. If you find that you simply cannot add one more thing to your plate, or that your parent requires daily monitoring, or that you live in another state or on the other side of the country, then if you have the means you may want to hire a geriatric care manager. (Their fees range between $50-$200/hour.)

A geriatric care manager (GCM) is a professional with specialized knowledge and expertise in senior care issues. (See page 158 for a full description.)

Step 8 — How to navigate delicate waters.

For years, my mother said that she hoped she would die in her sleep. This is what most of us would like. After all, if given a choice, we wouldn't sign up for a long protracted decline. But the reality is that only a small percentage of people die suddenly. The vast majority of us will have to deal with end-of-life issues.

As your parent ages, it is important to know what she wants you to do in case she becomes incapacitated or suffers a life-threatening event. Does she want to be resuscitated regardless of the situation, or only under certain circumstances? If your parent does not have a Do Not Resuscitate (DNR) order and has an event, such as a heart attack, that requires cardiopulmonary resuscitation (CPR), it will be administered. However, what you and your parent must know is that survival statistics for people who receive CPR in their 80s and 90s are grim. A 2002 study published in the journal *Heart* found that <u>fewer than 2%</u> of people in this age group who had been resuscitated for cardiac arrest at home lived for one month.[6] If your parent, like the vast majority of seniors, wants to die at home, then she should be amenable to having a DNR.

We live in a culture that touts that everything that can be done will or should be done. Often life-altering decisions are made in haste instead of having heart-to-heart discussions that look at the bigger picture, that examine the odds and provide realistic expectations and consequences of certain procedures.

Does she want a DNR?

Depending on her frailty or if she is in palliative care or hospice, your parent may want a DNR. If she is fortunate to be at home while facing her final days, a DNR will provide some assurance that she will not end up in an emergency room or end up dying in an ICU or hospital. A DNR can be obtained from her primary care physician. Typically it is kept on the refrigerator, but unless your parent is bedridden, I would suggest that it be kept elsewhere. No one needs to be reminded that death could be right around the corner.

Bringing up this topic can be difficult for everyone. It obviously is easier when a parent is in hospice or is terminally ill.

Because my mother had an incurable type of anemia for several years, her doctor recommended that she have a DNR. Depending on your parent's state of health, when the time comes it may be wise for her doctor to bring up this topic.

Once you have entered these delicate waters, you might also want to explore other topics that are often not discussed, such as final arrangements that have not yet been made. For some families, such discussions are seen as taboo. However, once you have broached the topic of a DNR, it is a natural segue to talk about final arrangements. Does your parent want to be buried or cremated? If she does not have a burial plot, where would she like to be buried? Does she want to be an organ donor? Does she want to participate in the writing of her obituary? For ways of gently approaching this topic, see Chapter 4, "Talking about death is not taboo."

CHAPTER 2

A Comprehensive Approach Including New Technologies

Staying healthy and fit are key to maintaining independence

With obesity, diabetes, and heart disease on the rise, we all need to take greater responsibility for our health. Many diseases are preventable if only we would adhere to a reasonable diet and follow an exercise program. And, although the sooner we engage in healthy eating and exercise the better, it is never too late to start.

All sorts of books have been written about how we can lose weight, improve blood sugar levels, and reverse chronic conditions such as heart disease. However, once a condition has become chronic, it is more difficult to change its course than if one had prevented it in the first place. Most of us are painfully aware of how difficult it is to lose weight, a challenge that becomes even more difficult as we age.

Quite a few years ago, I read "Dean Ornish's Program for Reversing Heart Disease," and even though I have been a vegetarian for nearly four decades, I would not have been able to follow his severely restricted diet. Perhaps if my choices were to follow his program or do nothing and die, I might have been motivated. Moderation seems to be the key, both in terms of how much we eat and how much we exercise. When we are presented with severe choices, we set ourselves up for failure.

Learning about nutrition and making healthy food choices, eating foods that provide essential nutrients, and committing to some sort of daily physical activity is all that is really necessary to improve one's physical and mental health.

We are what we eat

The next time you are at your parent's house, see what she has in her refrigerator and pantry. It might be wise to set a time to review the ingredients on labels of packaged foods and drinks and point out the dangers of trans fats, artificial sweeteners, preservatives, etc. Trans fats (also known as trans fatty acids) are found in foods such as vegetable shortening, some margarines, crackers, candies, baked goods, cookies, snack foods, fried foods, salad dressings, and many processed foods. It is important to know about trans fats because there is a direct relationship between diets high in trans fat content and high LDL ("bad") cholesterol levels. Elevated cholesterol levels are a risk factor for coronary artery disease. If the ingredient list includes the words "shortening," "partially hydrogenated vegetable oil," or "hydrogenated vegetable oil," the food contains trans fat and should be avoided. If your parent already suffers from coronary artery disease, eliminating trans fats from the diet could prove to be very beneficial.

You may also want to share with her the benefits of healthy fats like the omega-3 and omega-6 fatty acids found in oily fish, oils, nuts, and avocados. Omega-3 and omega-6 fatty acids benefit the hearts of healthy people as well as those at high risk for or who have been diagnosed with cardiovascular disease. Omega-9 is another fatty acid that does not get as much press as omega-3 and omega-6. Omega-9 is found in olive oil and nuts, and lowers cholesterol levels. It also reduces the risk of atherosclerosis (hardening of the arteries), reduces insulin resistance and improves glucose (blood sugar) stability, improves immune function, and provides protection against certain types of cancer.

If your parent has high blood pressure, reducing the consumption of foods high in salt can be extremely helpful. Government guidelines recommend that people consume less than 2,300 milligrams of sodium per day — or about 800 milligrams of sodium per meal. Foods classified as high-sodium foods contain more than 400 milligrams per serving. The obvious foods to avoid are pretzels, potato chips, crackers, salted nuts, popcorn, corn chips, etc. But most people are unaware of how much salt lurks in canned soups, processed cheeses, hot dogs, bacon, lunch meat, frozen meals, sauce and gravy mixes, stuffing, soy sauce, bouillon cubes, and other processed foods. Even cottage cheese, which seems so bland, is loaded with salt. So just cutting back on salt by not adding it to homemade meals may not be enough if your parent has high blood pressure or suffers from congestive heart failure.

A diet high in fiber with plenty of fresh fruits and vegetables, whole grains, nuts, and cereals such as oatmeal, plus plenty of good drinking water, will keep your parent healthier longer.

A glass of red wine a day can be healthy, but. . .

My mom liked the occasional cocktail, around 5:00 or so in the evening, but after she was widowed at the age of 88, she did not like to drink alone. From time to time she would indulge, particularly if a neighbor or a friend had come over to chat. However, by the time she was in her 90s, she was taking some prescription medications that clearly stated that alcohol was to be avoided. It is important to pay close attention to these warnings, as combining alcohol with certain drugs can produce unpleasant side effects.

Because most older seniors take five or more medications a day, it is important to see what the warnings are regarding alcohol. If there are no restrictions, there is nothing wrong with a glass of red wine or even a cocktail once a day. After all, some say a glass of red wine a day can help raise HDL, the good cholesterol.

The multiple benefits of exercise

Staying active is one of the best ways to maintain muscle integrity, joint flexibility, and balance, and to live independently longer. Depending on the health of the individual, different types of exercise can be performed. Seniors who are fit and have received a clean bill of health from their doctor can engage in aerobic activity, which offers numerous health benefits for the body and the mind. Aerobic exercise increases endorphins, which in turn enhance the immune system and lift our spirits. Exercise can be a wonderful antidote to depression. It also improves the cardiovascular system, thereby benefiting circulation and heart health by increasing HDL (good cholesterol) levels and reducing LDL (bad cholesterol) levels. Exercise can also lower blood pressure and reduce weight or help maintain a healthy weight. It increases joint mobility and improves muscle tone. Whenever an aerobic program is started, it should be started gradually, exercising just a few minutes a day and increasing the length of time in small increments until the goal is reached.

And yes, walking can be boring. If your parent has a headset or an iPod, it may add some interest. If she lives out in the country where the landscape is forever changing, being one with nature can be a great experience without the distraction of music or talk radio. Sharing a walk with nature's critters and bearing witness to the wonder brought about by seasonal changes can have the added benefit of being uplifting and at times even spiritual. But if walking is not an option or not desired, then perhaps your parent may want to try certain low-impact sports such as bowling or golf, even if for only nine holes.

My mother learned to play golf at the age of 76! Her second husband, whom she married when she was 72 years old, was a golfer. She had never played golf, but in her youth had been quite a good tennis player and therefore had pretty good hand-eye coordination. Because her husband thought it would be fun for both of them if she could join him on the golf course, he bought her a set of clubs and some lessons for her 76th birthday. Much to everyone's surprise, she was a natural. In fact, she became so good that she was on the winning team at their local club, and her name is memorialized on a bronze plaque — something that her husband never succeeded in accomplishing even after having played on the same course for decades.

The other advantage of playing sports is that it provides an avenue for socializing. My mother and stepfather would go out to dinner with other couples from the golf club. My stepfather was also a member of a men's bowling league that bowled a couple of times a week. Afterwards, they would go out for coffee. This gave him a chance to hang out with the "boys," and it also gave my mother a little space. It probably did both of them a world of good. He played on the league until his mid-80s.

Several years ago, I saw a documentary about a woman in her mid-80s who had arthritis and was becoming more and more immobile. She became concerned because she lived alone and feared that at the rate she was going, she would soon be relegated to a wheelchair and condemned to a not-too-pleasant life. She asked her physician what she could do and he recommended that she exercise.

From the time she was a young girl, this woman had always wanted to take ballet. Although she lived in New

York City, where one can find almost anything, she knew that it was unlikely that she would find a ballet class of her peers. So she came to terms with her choices and joined a class of young women in their 20s. And even though she could not bend as far as the young dancers could, over time she became more flexible and mobile and less fearful about what the future held.

There are exercise classes for seniors at local YMCAs and senior centers. My mother attended one until her early 90s, when she developed mild dysplastic anemia and no longer had the strength to exercise. Classes for seniors are geared for those who do not have great stamina and cannot bend themselves into a pretzel. After her class, my mother always came home recharged and full of energy.

For seniors who no longer drive or have difficulty finding transportation, there are DVDs, which can be viewed at home, and which demonstrate how to use light weights and exercise bands, how to stretch, etc. And if they want something more active and fun, Nintendo's Wii system offers all sorts of wonderful virtual games. These games are being used by physical therapists across the country, with some physical therapists calling them "Wiihabilitation." Unlike boring repetitive exercises, the games are mentally engaging and enjoyable. The most popular Wii games in rehab involve sports: baseball, bowling, boxing, golf, and tennis. Using a wireless controller, players direct the actions of animated athletes on the screen. Wii also offers aerobic exercises and dance instruction that some seniors might enjoy as well.

Exercises that may help reduce the incidence of falls

"The great secret that all old people share is that you really haven't changed in seventy or eighty years. Your body changes, but you don't change at all."
– Doris Lessing, British writer (1919-)

Numerous studies confirm that older adults value their independence and fear that, if they should become disabled, they may not be able to remain in their homes. According to the CDC, more than one-third of people 65 years of age and older fall each year, and those who fall once are two to three times more likely to fall again. Fall injuries are responsible for significant disability, reduced physical function, and loss of independence. Because falls can be so debilitating, it is important to look at ways to prevent them.

Our parent still may be young at heart, but as the years march on, muscle tone and muscle mass decrease. The joints become stiffer, and the stamina once enjoyed seems to vanish. Coming to terms with physical limitations can be challenging. On the inside, she still feels young and reminisces about the days of her youth, fondly remembering when she was a superstar able to serve an ace at nearly 100 miles an hour or hit a 250-yard drive down the fairway. But her body no longer wants to cooperate. Tasks that once were taken for granted, such as cleaning under the bed or climbing a ladder, become challenging over time. The knees no longer bend like they used to, and climbing a ladder requires balance and agility, which are often compromised as old age sets in. As the years pass by, you may notice that your parent starts to shuffle a bit. Her stance might widen or her balance may become shaky — signs that she has become more vulnerable. This can be an accident waiting to happen.

Fortunately there are exercises to help strengthen muscles and restore balance, thus minimizing the incidence of falling. Yoga, tai chi, and Pilates all promote endurance, strength, flexibility, and balance.

Yoga: Yoga is an ancient art based on harmonizing the body, mind, and spirit. It achieves balance by holding poses. The downward-facing dog and the triangle, two fairly popular poses, may help elders strengthen muscles and learn new ways to balance, thereby fending off falls. A study from Temple University's School of Podiatric Medicine suggests that Iyengar yoga, a type of yoga involving props like belts, ropes, and cushions, could prevent falls among people 65 years old and older. After nine weeks of training, older women showed improvement in their balance and had greater range of motion and flexibility in their legs and feet. Researchers noted that it appeared that their weight was more evenly distributed throughout the foot, which can result in improved stability and decrease the likelihood of falling.[5]

Tai chi: Even though yoga may help with balance, some researchers believe that tai chi and Pilates are more effective at improving motor control and coordination for walking, which is when most falls occur. Originating in China 2,000 years ago, tai chi consists of slow, smooth movements that bring calm and clarity to the mind. When done correctly, it also improves muscle tone, flexibility, balance, and coordination. Many seniors who practice tai chi have said that it improves their energy, stamina, and agility. Numerous studies have demonstrated the benefits of tai chi with regard to preventing falls among the elderly. One study enrolled a group of fall-prone senior citizens with an average age of 78 who were living in residential care. Twenty-nine study subjects attended a 12-week tai chi course three times a week, and 30 control subjects did not exercise. The study found that subjects in the tai chi group were more physically fit than those in the control group and showed significant improvement, with stronger knee and ankle muscles, improved mobility and flexibility, and better balance.[6]

Pilates: Pilates, named after Joseph Pilates, was originally created to provide greater strength and flexibility for dancers. It focuses on strengthening the core muscles of the abdomen, which support the back and enhance balance. The exercises also engage back and buttock muscles. By strengthening the hip and leg joints and the body's core (the abdominal and back muscles), seniors can reduce their risk of falling. Over time, Pilates can improve posture (some people feel that it makes them taller), improve balance, and increase bone density. Joseph Pilates practiced it well into his 80s, so it can be appropriate for almost any age.

A cautionary note: Osteoporosis, a weakening of the structure of the bone, is a special concern for seniors in Pilates, as it is with many fitness systems. Anyone at risk of osteoporosis should get a bone density scan before proceeding with Pilates practice. Weight-bearing exercises are often recommended as part of a bone-building program to prevent osteoporosis. However, a person who has been diagnosed with osteoporosis needs to avoid some of the forward-bending and back extension exercises that are part of the Pilates regimen.

Older adults with lower back problems, bad knees, osteoporosis, or other disabilities should consult with their doctors before signing up for a yoga, tai chi, or Pilates class.

Another modality that could help prevent falls is Feldenkrais®, which offers lessons called Awareness through Movement (ATM) and Functional Integration (FI). ATM and FI gently coax one's muscles and neurological makeup into remembering how they once functioned before there was a problem. Feldenkrais offers a broad spectrum of lessons (over 4,000) for a wide range of ailments and issues. For preventing falls, there are lessons that help lower the center of gravity. The lower our center of gravity, the more grounded we are to the earth and the less likely we will fall. Through observation, we know that people who have long legs and a short torso are more inclined to fall than those who have short legs and a long torso, as the center of gravity in the long-legged individual is higher. We cannot change our physique, but we can change where the center of gravity resides.

In addition to lowering the center of gravity, a Feldenkrais practitioner sorts out how each person is biased in creating balance. Vision and how we use our eyes, the sense of the orientation of one's limbs in space (proprioception), and the vestibular system all play a role in maintaining balance.

Feldenkrais lessons can expand the sensing skills in underused areas.

Another key component of the Feldenkrais method regarding balance is the importance of understanding rolling, a skill I was able to use recently. I am a senior myself and have been working with this method for 12 years because of chronic back issues. Over the years, I have learned lessons that have prepared my body to know intuitively what to do if I should fall. A few months ago, I inadvertently stepped backward into a culvert that was about 2 feet deep. As I stepped backward, I was immediately aware that I no longer was on *terra firma*, and somehow my body knew to twist into a spiral. So instead of landing on my coccyx, which would have been devastating to my back, I twisted my body in mid-air and gently landed on my knees. I must say I was totally surprised by the experience. I dusted myself off and was no worse for wear.

Bone up on vitamin D

When it comes to bone health, calcium is top of mind. After all, we've been encouraged to drink milk and consume foods high in or enriched with calcium to build good bones since childhood. However, vitamin D is equally important in preventing bone loss and fracture, as it is needed to properly absorb the calcium we ingest. Vitamin D also helps maintain normal blood levels of phosphorus, another bone-building mineral. Therefore, consuming adequate amounts of calcium and vitamin D may help prevent falls that otherwise might occur because of brittle bones.

Researchers have discovered that vitamin D plays a role far beyond just keeping our bones healthy. It is also believed to ward off a range of diseases, including cancer, hypertension, and diabetes. As these findings are recent, it will be interesting to keep on top of the latest developments.

How much vitamin D do we need? Some experts believe that adults should take 800-1,000 International Units (IU) of supplemental vitamin D daily to adequately prevent bone loss and possibly protect against cancer and other chronic diseases. Another approach is to take a larger dose less frequently. A single weekly dose of 5,000 IU or a single 100,000 IU dose once every few months could be an alternative. A clinical trial in the United Kingdom gave elderly men and women 100,000 IU of vitamin D every four months for five years. The subjects' rate of first fracture was 22% lower than those who were given a placebo, and they had a 33% lower fracture rate of the hip, wrist, and vertebrae.[7]

The sun can be our friend — and is another source of vitamin D

For years we have been warned about the harmful effects of the sun. If we want to avoid skin cancer and wrinkles, we must stay out of the sun. If your parent finds that she needs to be in the sun for an extended period of time, she should lather her skin with sunscreen — the higher the SPF, the better. Today, scientists and doctors tell us that getting some sun, preferably in the early morning or late afternoon, is one of the best sources of vitamin D (although how much the skin absorbs depends on skin tone, and is directly proportional to how close you live to the equator). The sun is still the primary cause of melanoma, so your parent should bask in the sun wisely and not for too long. Depending on your parent's skin tone, 10-20 minutes during the early morning or late afternoon might be enough. Unless your parent lives in a state where there is an abundance of sun during most days of the year, vitamin D supplementation is advised.

Another important benefit of sunlight is that it increases the production of melatonin, which regulates the body's sleep-wake cycle. For people who live in northern climes, where the days are short during the winter months, or in regions that are more cloudy than sunny, melatonin reserves can be depleted, as daytime darkness causes the hormone to be released during waking hours. Normally there are just traces of melatonin in the body during the day, but the body is fooled when there is darkness instead of light. When melatonin circulates in the blood during the day, it can make people feel less energetic and drowsy. Adding insult to injury, the daytime release depletes the body's reserves needed for sound sleep. A lack of a sufficient supply of melatonin during the night can result in fitful sleep or insomnia. Light therapy can help when natural sunlight is not available. However, the best way to keep melatonin levels balanced is by allowing natural sunlight to penetrate the skin — 20 minutes of sunlight on as much of the body as possible is all that is needed.

Emotional health — help her find her passion so she can have some fun

"In youth, the days are short and the years are long. In old age, the years are short and days long."
— Nikita Ivanovich Panin

Many elders find that time moves too slowly. The days can be painfully long and uninteresting. For some, the lingering passage of time can add to their sense of loneliness and accentuate their depression. Finding a hobby or something to fill the hours can certainly benefit one's mental health.

If your parent once played a musical instrument, she may want to pick it up again. Or perhaps she is an avid reader and would enjoy being a member of a book club. Maybe she always wanted to play chess. Many senior centers have chess clubs where some of the more seasoned members can teach those new to the game. Bridge and other card games, or even working on the same jigsaw puzzle can provide avenues for socializing and companionship.

My mom had always wanted to paint. Not having had any formal training in oil painting, she signed up for a painting class, which she attended for at least a decade. She became fairly good, considering her late start in life. She never got to the point where she could paint scenes from her head, but she enjoyed copying images from calendars, postcards, or books. The little church down the road from her home had an annual exhibit of local artists, and she always managed to sell a few of her paintings. She was fortunate in that she enjoyed several activities which helped the time pass by quickly.

If your parent has no interest in hobbies, there are other activities that she may want to explore. For example, if she is mobile, helping others is one of the best treatments for depression and loneliness. She may find activities such as stroking preemies at the local hospital, answering phones and helping with fundraising for a local charity or aid organization, or collecting signatures for a worthy cause, to be appealing.

The benefits of meditation

Over the years, meditation has been recognized as a major antidote to stress. It is used in clinical settings, hospitals, and pain clinics, and people from all age groups can benefit from its calming effects. Many retirement communities offer meditation classes for their residents. There are numerous types of meditations, including walking meditations. Some meditations are traditionally Eastern, whereas others have been adapted to better serve the Western mindset. Having a preference for one form over the other is quite personal. Some people enjoy silent meditations, meditations of soothing music, or meditations that just focus on the breath, while others prefer those that are guided. Many of the well-known holistic health gurus such as Deepak Chopra, Carolyn Myss, Dr. Andrew Weil, and others lead their own meditations, which are available on CDs.

Help for the caregiver too

Caregivers all too often find themselves stretched to the max as they are pulled in many directions, dividing their time between work and their own families and caring for their elderly parents. Fortunately there are numerous resources, including books and Web sites, that address topics such as how to prevent burnout, how to divide responsibilities among siblings, how to deal with siblings who are not carrying their weight, how to ask for help, how to find help, and what to do when you feel guilty or resentful, etc.

Since chronic stress can be an underlying cause of many ailments, finding the stress management tool that works for you is key to staying healthy. Some of us find that vigorous physical activity is a stress buster. If that works for you, take a jog, go for a swim, or jump rope — whatever you can fit into your schedule. Getting your circulation going and your endorphins flowing will make you feel better physically and mentally and may even help you get a good night's sleep.

For others, a less physically demanding way to unwind is what is needed. If you have any free time, even just 10 minutes a day, a leisurely walk in the woods or swinging on a porch swing or hammock will provide you with a little respite from life's demands. Perhaps finding a quiet place inside your house or in some secluded area nearby where you can meditate would also be beneficial. Another great de-stressor is a hot bath scented with lavender oil. After 20 minutes, the muscles relax, and the mind takes a minibreak from the stresses of daily life. Lavender has a calming effect on the mind and has been known to induce sleep when sleep seems evasive.

Remember: If you are the glue that is keeping it all together, then you must take the time to take care of yourself.

Laughter is free medicine

"You don't stop laughing because you grow old. You grow old because you stop laughing."
                                        – Michael Pritchard

Scientific studies have shown that laughter heals the mind and the body. Perhaps the most famous incident of using laughter for therapeutic purposes is the story of Norman Cousins, who wrote "Anatomy of an Illness." One could say that he is responsible for putting laughter into the healing repertoire. After leaving a hospital and checking into a hotel, Cousins watched videos of the Marx Brothers and Candid Camera and took large doses of vitamin C. He found that several hours of intense laughter alleviated his pain for a few hours at a time and he could finally catch some desperately needed sleep. Armed with just laughter and vitamin C, he recovered from a potentially fatal disease. When we laugh, the body releases endorphins, which act like our own internal supply of morphine. And unbeknownst to Cousins, endorphins also boost the immune system. Because hearty laughter affects the body's chemistry positively in ways similar to exercise, Cousins referred to it as "inner jogging".

Many studies, including those of Dr. Lee Berk and Stanley Tan of the Loma Linda University of Medicine in California, have documented that laughter has the opposite effect of stress on our physiology. It lowers cortisol and increases the production of endorphins. Elevated cortisol levels suppress the immune system and cause blood pressure to rise. Laughter, on the other hand, lowers cortisol levels and increases natural killer cells and T-cells that attack viruses and even some cancer cells.[8]

As adults, we do not laugh nearly enough. Toddlers laugh 300-400 times a day. By the time we reach adulthood, we laugh only about 15 times a day. My stepfather had a gift for remembering and telling jokes. He garnered most of his material from *Reader's Digest,* which he read religiously. And even though he often repeated the same jokes over and over, he would laugh as if it were the first time he had told them. He was quite healthy until he was 89 and passed away the following year. Clearly, people who can laugh at jokes, and even at themselves, probably are enjoying life a bit more than those who fail to see the funny side of life. With that said, it is important to recognize that we are all wired differently, and not everyone shares the same sense of humor. It seems that as we age we can get into a place where we take life too seriously. So if you can encourage your parent to lighten up a bit, you will be doing her a favor.

Herbs and supplements — something to think about

DISCLAIMER: The information provided below is intended for educational purposes ONLY and is NOT intended to suggest or recommend treatment. If you are interested in researching various conditions, go to http://www.nchi.nih.gov/pubmed and type one or two key words in the search box. You can search numerous conditions and supplements. Before you recommend that your parent take an herb or supplement, ALWAYS consult her physician first. Better still, find a physician who believes in holistic medicine.

A study presented at Yale University School of Medicine showed that more than 90% of seniors taking five or more medications experience one or more "mildly bothersome" side effects. One-third of study subjects attributed changes in mood, insomnia, impaired balance, fatigue, or dizziness to one or more of their medications.[9]

The Food and Drug Administration (FDA) has published a list of drugs that do not interact well with each other. To find out which drugs cause problems when taken together, you can do a search on http://www.drugs.com. For example, when searching Lasix®, a diuretic often given to patients with high blood pressure or edema due to congestive heart failure, *hundreds* of drugs are listed that may cause modest to severe interactions. With such a large inventory of drugs, it is not surprising that seniors who take multiple prescriptions experience side effects.

One way to help minimize side effects is to find alternatives such as supplements, herbs, or natural remedies. If you decide to go this route, you *must* work with a physician who is open to this approach, because some herbs and remedies can also cause side effects when combined with certain medications. As a medical writer and someone who has studied alternative healing methods for several decades, my bias has always been to find a supplement, herb, or homeopathic remedy that will achieve the same effect as a prescribed drug but is free of side effects.

When my mother was 94, she was diagnosed with lymphoma. She had a rather unusual presentation, as her tumors were external and on her left leg. Because of her age, she and I agreed that she would not undergo chemo-therapy. Instead, she took a 4-week course of Rituxan®, an antibody specific for her type of lymphoma. She also underwent radiation and took supplements to boost her immune system. In addition to her oncologist, we worked with a holistic physician, who recommended that she take maitake mushroom extract and IP-6, both immune enhanc-ers. After just two months of therapy, she was completely cured, and the tumors never returned.

An alternative remedy proved helpful during another occa-sion when my mother was near the end of her life. She was experiencing a fair amount of anxiety that would escalate until she was gasping for breath. While she was in the hos-pital recuperating from a broken pelvis, she was given Hal-dol® and Ativan® for anxiety. Both of these drugs made her paranoid and caused hallucinations. Because she realized that she was nearing the end of her life, and because she was afraid to die, anxiety became a problem. When she eventually went into rehab and experienced anxiety, her nurse, who was amenable to alternatives, gave her Rescue Remedy®, a Bach® flower remedy prepared similarly to homeopathic remedies. Rescue Remedy alleviated her anxi-ety but without the horrible side effects of Haldol and Ati-van. We used Rescue Remedy to treat her anxiety until she passed away.

I have many more stories, but you get the idea. The follow-ing is an example of how a supplement that is equally effec-tive can be substituted for a prescription drug.

Statins have a proven track record of lowering cholesterol but for some, the side effects are too high a price to pay. A study by Becker et al. found that lifestyle changes combined with ingestion of red yeast rice and fish oil reduced LDL-C (the bad cholesterol) in proportions similar to standard therapy with Zocor® (simvastatin). Red yeast rice is one of the primary ingredients of Zocor, so it stands to reason that it would be as effective, and it costs a fraction of what Zocor costs.[10] (This citation refers to clinical trials in which the efficacy of supplements was compared with prescribed drugs.)

Because statins inhibit the production of Co-Q-10, an enzyme essential for heart health, if your parent takes a statin, you may want to talk with their doctor about Co-Q-10 supplementation. Many clinical studies recommend Co-Q-10 supplementation when statins are prescribed.

The list of studies that compare supplements or herbs with prescription medications is growing by leaps and bounds as interest in treating ailments more naturally continues to grow.

21st century technologies provide a paradigm shift and offer more choices and cost savings

As our parents age, they will need some kind of assistance to remain independent. Already there is a shortage of CNAs, and this shortage will become significantly worse, as baby boomers will be drawing from the same pool. As this wave of rapidly aging Americans arrives, those who want to enter retirement communities, assisted living, or nursing home facilities will simply swamp existing places. The most logical solution, which also turns out to be the most cost-effective, is to find more ways to help our society age in place.

With such an onslaught of seniors needing services, the market is ripe for high-tech innovations and alternatives. Experts on aging say motion sensors and other high-tech devices will allow older people to live independently longer. Digital lifestyle technologies are slowly being adopted by the elderly, allowing them to stay longer in their own homes. They also can lighten the burden of care-givers and ultimately reduce health care costs.

"Big Brother" at his best — passive monitoring devices can give you and your parent peace of mind

When George Orwell wrote *Nineteen Eighty Four* in 1949, he probably never imagined that the phrase he coined, "Big Brother is watching you", would become a household phrase. Used ubiquitously by governments here and abroad as well as by companies who make sensors, the term "Big Brother" is applied to almost any sensor that records everything in its view 24/7. Today these sensors can make a world of difference in the quality of your parent's life, as they provide a gateway to maintaining independence.

Passive monitoring systems allow aging seniors to stay in their homes longer and grow old with dignity. A variety of monitoring options are available and include the installa-tion of motion sensors and a remote monitoring system that sends data to the caregiver and the system provider.

Changes in the senior's activities are analyzed so caregivers can be alerted to problems by call center professionals via e-mail, cell phone, text message, or pager, or by checking a password-protected Web site. Some of these systems, such as QuietCare®, "learn" what the normal behavioral patterns are and note any significant changes from what was observed initially.

Wireless sensors are usually mounted on the walls in or near the bathroom, bedroom, front door, kitchen, and other high-traffic areas. Most sensors detect motion, but others also monitor actions, such as if the door to the medicine cabinet has been opened or if the door to the refrigerator or room opens or closes. A pressure pad on the bed can tell if someone is resting or if the individual has been resting too long, signaling that there may be a problem. Data is sent via computer to family members, who can monitor the activities of their parent — did she get out of bed on time, how much time was spent in the bathroom, did she stop by the med box? When the system senses something wrong, it tries to reach someone on the list of emergency contacts, including family, friends, and neighbors. If no one is available, it will alert an emergency dispatcher.

Some parents may be resistant at first, but once they understand that it will help them maintain their independence longer, they usually embrace having such a system installed.

Although prices keep changing, the current fees are around $200-$1,000 for installation and activation plus a $40-$90 monthly fee. The fees vary according to company, size of system, and number of sensors. Another system, Simply-Home™, provides sensors that monitor doors, windows, and cabinets, as well as the stove (with a remote turn-off); medication management; the bed, floors, and chairs; and much more. More comprehensive monitoring is available and includes devices that can track blood pressure, weight, or respiration.

Both parents and their children agree that having a passive monitoring system gives them peace of mind, and it can reduce the strain and burden of the caregiver or adult child. The real beauty of this system is that caregivers can receive the information wherever they are. Even if they decide to take an overseas trip, something they may have been putting off because of concerns about their parent's well-being, they can now get daily reports wherever they happen to be. What freedom.

Other passive monitoring systems include Healthsense® and GrandCare®.

With a burgeoning aging population, new technologies are constantly being developed. To see a demonstration of what's on the horizon, check out the video on Center for Aging Services Technology's (CAST's) Web site at http://www.agingtech.org. It will introduce you to what high-tech health care will look like in the future and how health care will be monitored from a distance.

Blood pressure can be monitored from one's home

Currently there is a device that checks blood pressure with a cuff that automatically sends the reading to a monitoring center, which then notifies the doctor in charge of any changes. If the individual does not take her blood pressure at the designated time, the doctor's office will call and remind the patient to do so.

High-tech shirt detects falls

Scientists in Singapore have invented a high-tech shirt designed to notify family or friends if their loved one has fallen. (It is not yet available in the United States.) The shirt is fitted with an alarm in the form of a sensor-transmitter system. The ¾ inch × ¾ inch sensor is fitted near the pocket and can detect the speed and tilt of the wearer. A fall triggers the transmitter, which is a box the size of a credit card case attached to the bottom of the shirt. Using Bluetooth wireless technology, the shirt then sends a signal to a mobile phone or a computer, which will alert relatives or friends. This can be life saving, as the mortality rate due to complications from falls is quite high among seniors who are 65 years or older.

The LifeShirt® system may identify falls

Currently available in the United States, the LifeShirt (developed by Accenture Technology Labs in Chicago, IL) is a washable undershirt embedded with sensors that measure respiratory function, heart rate, posture, and activity. Collecting data on more than 30 physiologic signs, a recorder/transmitter sends the user's data to a remote command center and displays the results in real time to the patient. Baseline data and subsequent parameters are recorded prior to using the shirt. If an event occurs that falls outside the set parameters, an alert is sent automatically to a remote-care manager who can notify the patient's medical team if necessary. For example, the shirt can identify when a person has suddenly gone from standing to lying and remains motionless. Although the LifeShirt system has not yet been marketed to seniors, those living alone could benefit from its ability to detect falls.

Wireless remote bed alarm helps seniors needing assistance at night

Getting up during the night poses an additional risk for people who have balance issues. The Malem© Enuresis Wireless Remote Bed Alarm is a pressure-sensitive pad placed on the bed that alerts the caregiver with an audible alarm. A wireless signal is sent from the transmitter to a receiver when the person leaves the pressure pad, alerting the caregiver that the person needs assistance. Malem Medical provides other alarms that you may find useful. For example, they have an alarm called the Malem Sit Up Sensor, which can be clipped on to an article of clothing and help notify caregivers when a loved one who requires close monitoring has gotten up.

Amplified mobile phone doubles as an emergency response device

The ClarityLife C900™ is twice as loud as other cell phones and has large buttons for ease of use. Users can get help quickly by pressing the large red emergency button. The phone calls and sends text messages to five preprogrammed numbers, such as those of family, friends, neighbors, or emergency personnel. It cycles through the five contacts until someone picks up. This phone can be purchased for $185 and can be added to most existing mobile phone plans.

Check local providers for service. To order, visit http://www.clarityproducts.com/products/listing/item3289.asp

Electronic pillbox enhances compliance

In 2007, the National Council on Patient Information and Education (NCPIE) found that poor medication compliance costs the U.S. economy approximately $177 billion annually in direct and indirect costs. Compliance is an even bigger problem among the elderly, the majority of whom take more than five prescriptions a day. Noncompliance among the elderly has been associated with as many as 40% of nursing home admissions, according to the NCPIE.

New research demonstrates improved compliance when older adults who take medications are reminded by an electronic pillbox, which beeps indicating that it is time to take a pill and also announces how many pills to take. The interactive pillbox was tested among elder adults between the ages of 65 and 84 who were taking at least four different medications.

MedSignals® can hold up to a month's supply of medications and has separate compartments for up to four drugs. The box is programmed to beep at pill-taking times, indicate the appropriate compartment, and display the number of pills to take on a screen. When the lid is lifted, an audio message announces the number of pills to take and gives specific instructions about how to ingest the pill — with or without food, with a full glass of water, etc. The pillbox records a time stamp and transmits information from all of the open lids via phone lines to caregivers. There is a monthly charge for this type of system.

A similar device is MD.2 Personal Medication System, which gives verbal and text alerts, automatically dispenses pills, and monitors missed doses.

Prodigy® Voice helps diabetics who are visually impaired

Prodigy Voice allows the blind and visually impaired to check their blood glucose levels without assistance. This innovative device provides verbal readings of current and past glucose levels. Designed to be user-friendly, its repeat button allows users to replay the most recent reading as often as needed. Setting up the functions couldn't be easier, as a setup button audibly guides the user. The device uses a very small amount of blood and provides fast results; the test strip port has a prominent indentation to allow the user to easily locate the strip insertion point.

The Talking® Sign helps keep individuals with Alzheimer's safe

The Talking Sign, originally designed for the visually impaired, is a sensor that can be placed by a door and emits a prerecorded message such as "Don't touch the door" or "Turn around and come see me." The message will repeat itself until the person has moved out of range of the sensor.

The Ceiva digital photo frame may reduce isolation, loneliness, and depression

Even if your parent does not use a computer, she can still enjoy viewing digital photos. This device can be preloaded with up to 70 digital photos or be plugged into a home phone line to receive transmitted photos. Using the phone line (an optional feature at additional cost), the frame silently dials a local number each night to receive new photos e-mailed to the frame, without interruption to phone service or charges to the phone line. Seeing updated pictures of grandchildren, school plays, soccer games, and other activities, as well as loved ones, scenic shots, and family vacations can help your parent feel more connected and less isolated. To order, visit http://www.ceiva.com/cstore/ct/cstore_catalog.jsp

Take a peek at what's in the pipeline

There are a host of inventions in the pipeline, including wireless sensors and devices that regulate temperature, lights, and appliances, as well as sophisticated medical monitors.

Robots: they may not be warm and fuzzy, but they are the way of the future

With a rapidly aging society, robots may be the only solution to our health care crisis as a shortage of skilled nurses and CNAs continues to grow. Although relatively new to health care, robots have been working quite successfully in other arenas. In medicine, they are currently being used in emergency rooms and operating theatres. A number of surgical procedures are now performed by using robots, including new, less invasive prostate surgery resulting in better outcomes.

Researchers are exploring important issues about what functions a robot assistant could provide to seniors. They also are investigating how people react to robots that have more human-like characteristics. Long-term care facilities such as nursing homes and assisted living are exploring how to incorporate nanotechnology to improve the quality of life for seniors. In facilities using robots, the face of the physician appears on the screen in the robot's head, and a camera is positioned on top. The robot can be used to examine problems such as skin tears or exchange information with physicians. Staff members can also attend trainings and meetings without traveling. And in terms of helping nursing home residents, family members can "visit" remotely.

When we think of robots, many of us remember R2D2 or the more recent WALL-E. Probably very few of us ever envisioned that they would become part of our health care system. Fortunately for today's elderly and tomorrow's baby boomers, robots have come a long way.

The uBOT-5 is a robotic assistant being developed at the University of Massachusetts Amherst and is designed to help seniors who live alone. According to Rod Grupen, director of the Laboratory for Perceptual Robotics at UMass Amherst, "For the first time, robots have become inexpensive enough and safe enough to do meaningful work in a residential environment." Although the cost of building a single robot is prohibitively expensive (around $65,000), manufacturers estimate that once they are mass-produced they might cost only a couple of thousand dollars.

 When compared with what it costs to have a part-time, in-home caregiver ($19/hr × 12 hours × 7 days or $1,596 per week or $82,992 a year), the robot becomes a bargain.

The uBOT-5 is a small robot on wheels with a small footprint and has arms that can lift up to 2.2 pounds. It can navigate its owner's home, pick up articles that may have fallen, put away the groceries, and do housecleaning. Fitted with a Web camera, a microphone, and a touch-sensitive LCD display, it provides a gateway to the outside world. Being able to connect with others, in particular with family and close friends, may help alleviate some of the loneliness and depression felt by seniors who are often isolated. For example, a senior can take the robot's hand and lead it out to the courtyard, where she can have a virtual visit with her daughter and show off her prized roses, regardless of where she lives.

The robot is also a lifesaver. If its owner falls, the robot can ask her to smile, speak, or raise both arms, a movement the robot can demonstrate. This line of questioning is often used to determine if a person has had a stroke. If the individual is unresponsive, the uBOT-5 dials 911, then uses a digital stethoscope that transmits vital information to the paramedics. What better friend could we ask for?

Another robot whose development is well underway is Pearl the NurseBot, currently being developed by the People and Robots Project at Carnegie Mellon in conjunction with the University of Pittsburgh. Pearl can remind her owner to take medications, eat meals, visit the bathroom, or schedule medical appointments, and even relays TV schedules and weather forecasts. For people suffering from arthritis, robots are being designed to assist them in operating washers, dryers, microwaves, and ovens, in opening and closing the refrigerator door, etc. Developing a robot that is useful and friendly requires a deep understanding of humanity as well as breakthroughs in technology. As one researcher has said, "We have succeeded in helping people live longer; now we have to help them live better."

Another area in which there is a lot of interest is determining ways to help seniors prevent and detect falls. Here are a few examples of what is in the pipeline — the diversity and ingenuity of these devices are quite impressive:

A Magic Carpet — A "magic carpet" is on the drawing board that would measure changes in gait and thereby help avoid falls.

The iShoe — A new insole called the iShoe contains sensors that read how well a person is balancing, and will send out a signal if a person falls. The main objective is to gather data that analyzes patterns of how pressure is being distributed by the foot and to get a person to a doctor before a fall occurs. Once the data are available, it should be easy to train the elderly person to improve her balance through the use of physical therapy. The iShoe is currently being tested on about 60 people and is awaiting patent approval. The iShoe insole, which can be placed inside any shoe, will cost around $100.

The FallSaver® — The FallSaver is a small patch that attaches to the thigh, with a tilt sensor activated when the wearer stands up. This is most useful for seniors who need assistance. It signals the caregiver that the person has gotten up and alerts the wearer to sit back down until the caregiver can help them.

A gait-monitoring device — A gait-monitoring device is being developed at the University of Virginia. The device establishes a baseline, which is then measured against any deviations. When there is a change in gait, the caregiver and the senior are alerted that she may be at a greater risk for falling.

Guido™ the Smart Walker — Welcome to the world of robotics. Guido, a robotic walker, scans the room for tripping hazards and verbally cues the user that there is a problem ahead. If the user chooses to ignore the prompt, Guido automatically stops.

Wearable monitors — Wearable mobile medical devices will be able to detect dangerous cardiac events, obesity, and diabetes.

Memory aids — Autominder is a cognitive orthotic that provides users with reminders about their daily activities. Unlike simpler systems that only sound an alarm, Autominder is smart enough to make adjustments based on a client's behavior. For example, if the elder needs to be reminded to use the bathroom every three hours but she has gone on her own within the 3-hour window, Autominder automatically makes the adjustment and restarts the 3-hour clock. For some, Autominder could be used as an adjunct to in-home care; for others, it could be the first step before in-home care is introduced. In both cases it has great potential in helping the elderly with cognitive deficiencies to remain in their homes longer.

Intel® is working on a memory bracelet that vibrates at a specified time to remind the wearer of a medical appointment or to take medication.

Interactive monitoring devices — Cognitive Orthosis for Assisting Activities in the Home (COACH) is a system developed through the Intelligent Assistive Technology and Systems Lab (IATSL) at the University of Toronto. It helps people with dementia complete activities of daily living (ADLs) by providing an intelligent, supportive environment. Elders able to perform ADLs on their own can live more independently. Using a personal computer and a single video camera that unobtrusively tracks a user while performing an

ADL, COACH provides prerecorded (visual or video) cues to the user when necessary.

"uBox" intelligent pill dispenser — The uBox is a palm-sized intelligent pill dispenser that reminds an individual when to take her medication. It also keeps track of a patient's medication consumption so that double dosing can be avoided. For individuals who need to be monitored by a caregiver, uBox communicates with a cell phone via Bluetooth. The uBox offers a combination of critical features: locking, multi-pill dosage, and interaction tracking. The uBox is currently being field tested in India with 1,600 individuals with tuberculosis. When it becomes available, it will be offered at a price point that is a fraction of current solutions.

MIT's AgeLab is applying technology used by NASA in developing a "digital danskin" that may integrate biosensors to monitor health conditions like osteoporosis and other chronic diseases that may affect functioning. Their ongoing research is also investigating the application of telemedicine technologies that will someday manage chronic conditions such as congestive heart failure, diabetes, and obesity. For more information about exciting, innovative devices to help aging seniors maintain their independence, visit MIT's AgeLab at http://web.mit.edu/agelab and see what the future holds.

In-home caregivers — the mainstay in assisting seniors to age in place

Most family caregivers recognize when their parent needs assistance. However, convincing a parent that she needs assistance can be quite challenging. Elders often do not want someone intruding into their lives, and this is particularly difficult for a parent who is very private or choosy about whom they want to associate with. She may worry if she will like the care provider; she may feel that having a care provider is an imposition; all of a sudden there will be a schedule when before there was greater flexibility; and the list goes on. But if your parent has acknowledged that she is having difficulties with everyday living skills such as bathing, preparing meals, or bending to get the laundry out of the washer, it's time to have a heart-to-heart talk about in-home care.

Initially, your parent may need assistance for only a few days a week. At first she might be a bit prickly, raising her hackles of resistance. My mother was extremely resistant to the idea of having someone "invade her privacy." But, at 94 and no longer being as strong as she used to be, she finally agreed, and after a few weeks she actually looked forward to having an aide. Aging in place can be lonely, and in-home care workers can break up the monotony and provide a bit of companionship. If you find that in-home care is too hard on your budget, then combining it with some of the high-tech devices and support from your community may make caring for your parent more affordable.

Ask questions before you sign on the dotted line

Before you hire an agency, do your homework! Ask your neighbors and friends if they know someone who works in the home health care system or anyone who has hired an agency. This is always a good place to start. Get as many referrals as you can.

I had been referred to one agency that was in such demand that I could never get them to provide services. However, they recommended an agency, which I hired based on their recommendation. Unfortunately, I did not check any further and did not get references. In retrospect, I should have dug deeper, but hindsight is always 20/20.

Appendix A, Questionnaire for Screening In-Home Care Agencies, provides a comprehensive checklist to use when evaluating an in-home care agency.

If your parent is receiving 24/7 CNA coverage, the reality is that many different CNAs will be traipsing through the house. Some will be a better match than others. It is *highly likely* that neither you nor your parent will be happy with all of them. All you can do is hope that those who fit in best with your parent's needs and lifestyle will be assigned more often. Ask the agency if you can request certain individuals and if they honor such requests.

 When handed a contract, you can feel pressured to read it quickly and sign it. Always read the fine and not-so-fine print. Before you sign a contract, I encourage you to read it carefully. Remember, "the devil is in the details." When my mother needed only three hours of care a day, she had signed a contract with one of the in-home health care agencies (which I refer to as agency number 1). After she fractured her pelvis, her care was extended to 24/7, and she was placed in hospice. Not expecting to survive her fracture, she surprised everyone and recovered enough so that she needed to go into rehab. However, because I had never seen the original contract, I was unaware of their termination policy. After I had transferred my mother to rehab and suspended the contract, they informed me that they had a 2-week termination policy. As a result of my failure to give them this 2-week notice, they wanted to charge us an additional $2,600 (and actually sent us a bill) and could have charged us $6,250 for care that was never provided! I am happy to report that they lost their case. Termination clauses vary from agency to agency. In some cases it is just 24 hours; in our case it was two weeks. When you contract with an agency, make sure you know their termination policy.

Introducing in-home care gradually can give you and your parent a chance to assess whether the CNAs who have been assigned are a good fit and if you like working with the agency. Is the agency living up to your expectations, do they deal with criticism well, and are they able to troubleshoot when there is a problem?

In-home care providers can also be hired privately. Depending on your parent's needs, the person you hire does not necessarily have to be a CNA. If your parent has long-term care insurance, there may be a provision that allows for hiring whomever you want. That person can be a friend or someone from your parent's church, a neighbor, etc.

Working with an agency clearly has pros and cons. Likewise, there are advantages and disadvantages when hiring a private in-home care provider.

Pros and cons of hiring an agency versus privately hiring an in-home caregiver

Hiring a home health care agency

Pros: They do the background checks to see if the person has a criminal record and do all of the screening, training, and supervising of their staff. Their staff is bonded, and the agency is ultimately held accountable. They also are responsible for paying their staff, which includes handling the paperwork regarding taxes and social security. If one of the aides is sick or cannot work her shift, they will be able to provide a substitute. If your parent finds that a particular aide is objectionable, she should be able to find a replacement. In addition to providing CNAs, their staffing capabilities may include skilled nursing, occupational therapy, physical therapy, etc. The range of services varies among agencies, and some agencies may be covered in part by Medicaid or private insurance.

Cons: There is not as much consistency, as several workers are assigned. This can be confusing for your parent and can also lead to mistakes. The inconsistency can create frustration, as some aides are far more diligent than others. Some aides will stay busy all the time looking for work, while others will watch TV or sit at the kitchen table and just chat. If your parent becomes fond of a particular aide and that aide gets reassigned, it can be disappointing, and adjusting to a new aide can be difficult. Some agencies, however, are very sensitive to the importance of stability and work very hard to provide the same CNAs as often as possible.

Hiring CNAs through an agency is more expensive than hiring them privately.

Privately hiring an in-home caregiver

Pros: Because the same caregiver comes every day, a strong relationship can develop between your parent and the caregiver. Hiring privately usually is less expensive than using an agency. You also have more say as to who will be providing the care, as you will be the one to do the interviewing and screening and therefore will have control over who will be caring for your parent.

Cons: Before you hire the caregiver, you will need to do a criminal background check and get and check references. You also will need to draw up a contract. This contract should include:

- Wages
- Withholding tax
- When and how payment will be made

- Number of hours of work each week
- Designated holidays and subsequent rate increases
- Employee's social security number
- A job description clearly delineating the duties to be performed
- A termination policy describing how much notice needs to be given by either party
- Reasons for termination without notice
- Dated signatures by you and the employee.

If the caregiver has an emergency or gets sick, you will have to scramble to try to find someone else. If the caregiver is abusive toward your parent, you may not know, because there is no one supervising this person. In addition, if your parent is difficult or demanding, there is a greater chance for burnout, and the caregiver could just quit, leaving you high and dry.

How to find the right in-home caregiver

Finding the right person can be a challenge. A good place to start is to ask for a recommendation from relatives or friends. You could post an ad at your local churches, synagogues, senior centers, and colleges, especially ones that have schools of nursing or social work. A good resource is your local Area Agency on Aging, which can provide you with a list of home care agencies and suggestions for places to advertise in your community.

Once you hear from applicants, some of the screening can take place over the phone. This way you can weed out those who do not seem like a good fit. When interviewing applicants over the phone, explain the job duties in detail and go over hours and wages. Ask the applicant about past experience and request some references. If the applicant seems like someone you think would do a good job, set up an interview with your parent and yourself. If possible, invite another family member or friend in for a second opinion.

You may want to ask the following questions:

- How long have you worked in this capacity?
- Where have you worked before?
- What were your responsibilities?
- What did you like about your past jobs?
- What didn't you like about your past jobs?
- Why did you leave your last post?
- Have you worked with the elderly (disabled, memory-impaired, patients with Alzheimer's) before? (This question can be tailored to your needs.)
- Do you have a car? (If she will use her own car to transport your parent to appointments, then you should have a clause in the contract that you will reimburse her for travel.)
- Are you able to transfer someone from a wheel-chair into a car or into a bed?
- Have you been trained to assist with bathing?
- Have you had to cook for others before? Do you consider yourself to be a good cook?
- What is your availability? How many days and how many hours can you work?

- Can you provide references (minimum of two work-related and one personal reference)?

During the interview, observe how the potential hire interacts with you and your parent. Observe her body language and expressions during the interview process. Elicit feedback from any friends or family members who attend the interview with you.

Always check references. If the candidate pans out, then have them sign a contract in duplicate, so you each have a copy. Make sure to go over it line by line so you share the same expectations.

Responsibilities and considerations as an employer

There are several legal considerations when you have employees working in your home. Does your renter's or homeowner's insurance cover household employees in case of an accident? If not, you may want to talk with your carrier about adding some kind of liability coverage. As an employer, you are responsible for paying social security taxes for those in your employ. For information on paying federal taxes for household employees, call (800) TAX-FORM and ask for Publication 926, or look for it on the Web at http://www.irs.gov/formspubs/index.html. There may also be state regulations. To find out what your state requires, call the state employment department listed in the government section of your phonebook.

If necessary, you may want to consider filling out Employment Verification Form I-9, which verifies that a person is legally entitled to work in the United States. This form can also be obtained from the phone number and Web site cited above.

Other in-home options for a parent needing 24/7 care

Private, live-in, round-the-clock care — agency-provided or personally hired — can save you some money

There are some agencies that provide 24-hour care with just one CNA. This person lives in, is given room and board, and is paid around $850/week, a much less expensive alternative to three shifts a day at $19/hour or $3,192/week. This option has pluses and minuses. On the plus side, there is consistency, and the CNA gets to know your parent quite well. However, on the downside, what happens if your parent does not like this person, if this person is abusive, or gets sick or has a family emergency? Unless your parent is in hospice or palliative care, or has family or friends who visit on a regular basis, if abuse takes place, no one is there to report it. Also, most people need some downtime. Although live-in aides typically get eight hours off each week, in reality this is not very much time. It could be a recipe for burnout. And furthermore, who will take care of your parent during these hours?

Cost-$aving Tips

	National average	Yearly cost
Agency-provided live-in 24/7 in-home care	$850/week plus room and board	$44,200
Agency-provided 24/7 in-home care	$19/hr × 24 hours × 7 days = $3,192/week	$165,984

When I looked into this service, I was told that most of the providers did not have cars. Unless you are in an urban environment, how would this person be able to run errands? He or she could use the family car, if there is one, but then you must be sure that you are carrying the proper insurance and are comfortable with a stranger driving your parent's car.

Another option is finding a private provider. We actually found someone who initially was willing to take on this role. But upon further reflection, she became overwhelmed with having so much responsibility. There are legitimate concerns, such as the liability of the private provider if the patient falls or gets sick on his or her watch.

If you decide to hire someone on your own, make sure you get references, and have the individual provide you with a copy of the results of a police background check.

If you end up hiring a CNA, first check with your State Department of Health or Board of Nursing to see if that person is registered. Also ask if there is a way for you to find out if this individual has been reported for any wrong-doing.

Remember: If you hire someone on your own, you will be responsible for paying social security and Medicare taxes if you pay more than $1,200 in cash during the year. You can learn more about how to pay and report these types of wages by visiting http://www.ssa.gov and searching Household Workers. Regardless of whom you hire, be sure to get a signed contract similar to the one described previously under "cons" in the section "In-home caregivers."

> If you can find a 24/7 live-in provider that you trust and feel comfortable with, this is an option that is considerably less expensive than round-the-clock in-home agency care.

Novel community-based alternatives provide comfort at home and in home-like environments

For independent seniors, the Beacon Hill Village model and other community-based programs are popping up in the suburbs

The concept for Beacon Hill Village in Massachusetts was developed by MIT's AgeLab as a creative solution to help seniors age in their homes. Residents of the greater Beacon Hill area wanted to find a way to remain in their homes, grow old with their friends, be able to attend their concert series and keep their pets. For them, moving was not an option.

Beacon Hill Village was officially founded in 2002 after considerable research by members 50 years old or older living in Beacon Hill, the Back Bay, the West End, and nearby neighborhoods, who wanted to age at home with the help and support of their community.

Today, Beacon Hill Village has 460 members ranging from 51 to 99 years of age. The nonprofit group collects an annual membership fee of $600 for an individual or $850 for a household. For members of moderate means, lower rates are available. These dues go toward providing access to services such as home health care, wellness programs, home repair, cleaning, transportation, shopping, meals, a concierge service, and social activities. By having a comprehensive directory of services, most needs can be met (including unexpected, unusual requests such as helping a member get a cat into a carrier so she could take it to the vet).

Beacon Hill Village carefully vets all of the service providers on their referral list, and members receive discounts of 10-50% off their fees. The most frequent requests are for transportation and computer help. It should be noted that transportation requests are not just for doctors' appointments, but also include vacation destinations for the more active members who want to go to the Cape or to the mountains for a little skiing. These elders clearly are staying active.

Beacon Hill Village has sold its founders' manual to groups nationwide and has consulted with hundreds of groups. The model can be adapted to any suburban or rural area; however, most groups are in cities.

If you are interested in learning how to start such a community, visit http://www.stayingputnc.org to see how people in New Canaan, CT, started a community modeled after Beacon Hill Village. Alternatively, you can order a manual from http://www.beaconhillvillage.org.

Here are just a few suggestions adapted from Beacon Hill Village's Web site, http://beaconhillvillage.org, and printed with permission:

- Get to know your community — find out the number of elders, their needs, income, geographic area, what kinds of programs they need, and what is currently available.
- Identify people passionate about staying in their own homes, and form a core group. (This may require someone going door-to-door.)
- Purchase the Beacon Hill Village "How-To" manual.
- Conduct a survey to see who in your area is interested in participating in this venture.
- Contact health care and other providers. See if you can get discounts from vendors for your members.
- Identify people who may help with writing a business plan. Contact the Small Business Administration (SBA) or talk to retirees with a background in business.
- Make a list of folks who could fundraise in order to raise seed money.
- Create a board of directors.
- Hire a director who will work with the community and the board of directors.
- Attend a Beacon Hill Village workshop or conference.

Communities are becoming more creative in terms of finding ways to help their elderly neighbors

According to the American Association of Retired Persons (AARP), about 90% of retirees and 80% of baby boomers say they want to remain in their lifelong neighborhoods indefinitely.[3] To help their elderly neighbors, many communities are finding innovative ways to offer assistance, even in the suburbs. Some programs provide seniors with chefs and home repair services, grocery shopping, or rides to the doctor. Many communities are rich in resources, but people do not know how to access them or how they may qualify for them.

The first aging-in-place program began in Penn South, a 10-building apartment complex in Manhattan. It was created in 1986 in response to an 84-year-old tenant with dementia, who died from exposure on the roof of one of the buildings. Unlike Manhattan or other densely populated cities, creating such programs in the suburbs presents many challenges. Whereas apartment complexes house large numbers of people in tight, compact environments, seniors living in the suburbs usually live in single-family homes spread out over many streets and neighborhoods.

Another example of a successful aging-in-place program can be found in a suburb of Minneapolis where Jewish Family and Children's Services help the elderly age in their homes. Local seniors participate by helping each other with transportation to medical appointments and by putting together directories of home care agencies and other lists, such as one that identifies hair stylists who make house calls. Jewish Family and Children's Services discovered that once one agency got involved, the word spread. In Minneapolis, for example, other nonprofit agencies, businesses, and government agencies started a Community Chore Day to help their older residents with home maintenance chores. Further assistance is being provided by the local Rotary Club as well as by some local high schools.

If for some reason you and your parent simply cannot find a way to help her age at home, there are some novel residential alternatives that provide comfort, care, and a home-like environment.

The group home concept is being revisited

With the cost of assisted living, nursing homes, and in-home care out of reach for many of today's elders, a new model is emerging — that of the group home. The national average cost of a nursing home is between $67,000 and $78,000 per year. Round-the-clock, in-home care is more than double that, at $166,000 per year, based on the nation's average of $19/hour for a CNA.

Most elderly, even frail elderly, do not really need round-the-clock care. They usually need someone to help them with their medications, prepare their meals, get them out of bed, and help them with bathing and dressing. A one-to-three ratio of in-home health care aide to residents is more than adequate in terms of being able to provide for everyone's needs. In nursing homes, the CNA-to-resident ratio is often one to 10 or 12 residents and can be even higher.

If three elders moved into a house or an apartment together, instead of spending $78,000 per year each, they could pool their resources and hire a 24-hour aide for $166,000 and still have $88,000 left over among them for food, clothing, shelter, physical therapy, and (hopefully) some fun.

The Green House

Another residential alternative for elders who need skilled nursing is called a Green House. Green Houses provide a nurturing living space for 6-10 elders. They try to emulate a normal living environment, free from the regimentation typically seen in nursing homes. They are a radical departure from traditional skilled nursing homes and assisted living facilities, altering size, design, and organization to create a warm community. Their innovative architecture and services offer privacy, autonomy, support, enjoyment and a place to call home. In Green Houses, residents are given back some of their dignity. Household decisions are made jointly by seniors and the staff who take care of them.

Green Houses look and feel like a house. Often bedrooms are on the periphery of the building, with common space in a central location. All bedrooms are private and have a private bath. Elders can close their doors to indicate that they want privacy. The caregivers are CNAs, but are referred to as Shahbaz (a Persian word meaning royal falcon) and are considered to be "midwives of elderhood." Their mission is to protect, sustain, and nurture those in their care. They are trained to be habilitators who bring out abilities even in the frailest elderly. They are paid about the same as CNAs who work in nursing homes, but the biggest difference is the healing environment that touches the hearts of both the caregivers and those who are being cared for. In long-term care, love matters. Unlike the high turnover rate seen in nursing homes, typically around 100% over the course of one year, Green Houses boast a retention rate of almost 100%. The ratio of staff to residents is about one-third higher than in the average nursing home.

There are 20 active Green House projects in 16 states. During the next 5 years, 100 more will be developed. Frail elders go to Green Houses to live, not to die. The philosophy behind the concept of Green Houses is that everyone, regardless of frailty, can still continue to grow. Because of the love that is provided, many residents who were faring poorly when they first arrived can regain their strength, appetite, and zest for life.

Green Houses cost around $242/day, about the same as a nursing home. Medicaid pays all but $25 a day. Around two-thirds of Green House residents are eligible for Medicaid.

Granny flats/elder cottages — getting your parent to move "next door"

Seniors who are no longer able to continue living independently for either financial or physical reasons but do not yet require assisted living may want to look into having a "granny flat" placed on the property of one of their children or relatives. ECHO (Elder Cottage Housing Opportunities) provides a senior housing unit, which is basically a manufactured home. It is usually a small studio or a one-bedroom unit of 700 square feet or less.

The concept of elder cottages originated in Australia as an option for seniors who want to live near their families but not with them. It offers the best of both worlds. Seniors get the physical and emotional support they need without having to hire caregivers. They can stay in touch with their grandchildren and everyone in the extended family and yet retain their privacy.

These units are cost effective. According to the U.S. Department of Housing and Urban Development (HUD), companies in California and Pennsylvania offer 500 square foot one-bedroom units, completely installed, for around $25,000. In other areas, the cost might be more but leasing and financing options may be available.

Some of the challenges that can arise include zoning codes that regulate density and may prohibit the installation of mobile homes. Therefore, before considering this option it is important that you look into the zoning codes governing your area. Also, because these units tap into existing plumbing and sewer/septic systems, you may need to acquire permits before the unit can be hooked up.

If you do not want to purchase a granny flat or cannot afford one, some manufacturers may rent them. For many, this could be a more attractive alternative.

Medicare and Medicaid support alternatives to nursing home care

Nursing homes serve predominantly the frail elderly. In 2004, about 1.5 million people lived in nursing homes across the United States. Eighty-eight percent of nursing home residents are 65 years old or older, and 45% are 85 or older. Yet only 2% of Americans age 65-85 and 14% of Americans age 85 or older live in nursing homes.[11]

Although the number of certified nursing homes fell between 1985 and 2004 from 19,100 to 16,100, the number of beds has increased, as newer nursing homes are much larger. But in spite of greater capacity, nursing home populations are declining: the occupancy rate has dropped from 92% to 86%.[11] The decline in occupied nursing home beds will likely continue as elders increasingly choose less institutional options such as assisted living or aging at home with community-based services. Medicare now offers two programs that assist those who have chosen to remain at home: the Social Managed Care Plan (SMCP), and the Program of All-Inclusive Care for the Elderly (PACE). These programs are popular with many individuals who want to live at home and in their own community and are hoping to avoid nursing home care.

A SMCP is similar to a traditional managed care plan, and offers the frail elderly health care coordination that includes prescription drug benefits; chronic care benefits such as short-term nursing home care; and a full range of home-based and community-based services such as homemaker, personal care services, adult day care, respite care, and medical transportation. Depending on the particular plan, eyeglasses, hearing aids, and dental benefits may also be provided.

This model of care is relatively new to the market, and currently there are only four managed care plans participating in the SMCP — in Portland, Oregon; Long Beach, California; Brooklyn, New York; and Las Vegas, Nevada. Each plan has different requirements for premiums, and they all have co-payments for certain services. Visit http://www.medicare.gov/nursing/alternatives/SHMO.asp for more information.

The second program, PACE, provides a wide range of services to older seniors who are frail enough to meet their state's standards for nursing home care. PACE features comprehensive medical and social services that can be provided at an adult day health center, in the privacy of one's home, or at inpatient facilities. This program allows most people to remain at home while receiving the care they need. A team of health care providers assesses an elder's needs and creates a health care plan. Services are available around the clock. Medicare and Medicaid pay PACE a fixed monthly fee per enrollee, regardless of the services used. Depending on eligibility, seniors enrolled in PACE may have to pay a monthly premium. At this time, PACE is available in only 24 states — CA, CO, FL, HI, KS, LA, MD, MA, MI, MS, MT, NY, OH, OK, OR, PA, RI, SC, TN,TX, VT, VA, WA, and WI. For more information, visit http://www.cms.hhs.gov/pace/lppo/list.asp.

If your parent is fortunate enough to live in one of the four states participating in Medicare/Medicaid's **SMCP** or in one of the 24 states that offer the PACE program, she will be able to save quite a bit of money. Because Medicaid does not pick up the nursing home tab until one's financial resources are depleted, these programs are a huge cost savings, and your parent will be so much happier aging at home.

How to pay for their care

If your parent has long-term care insurance, some of her care may be covered, depending on the policy. However, most policies provide coverage for a limited number of hours per day for a limited number of years.

If your parent does not have long-term care insurance, one way to pay for home care is by using a reverse mortgage, which allows her to access funds from her home equity without tapping into her income-producing investments. This method has been gaining popularity over the last several years. However, given the cyclical and geographic variations in real estate, this may not be an option for everyone. You will need to assess how the housing market is faring in your area to see if this might be an option for your parent. (See Web sites listed in Appendix C regarding information about reverse mortgages.)

Veterans and their spouses may qualify for the Disability Pension for Aid and Attendance, which provides funds for in-home care.

Be creative. As mentioned earlier, a combination of electronic devices such as passive monitoring and an electronic pillbox; community services such as Meals On Wheels; volunteers from churches, synagogues, high schools, or schools of nursing and social work; and some in-home care can be much more affordable than relying solely on in-home care.

CHAPTER 3

Managing My Mother's Care: Practical Tips

We never expect the unexpected

My 95-year old mother, who was sharp as a tack, had lived independently all of her life. She was widowed the first time in 1969 and then remarried at the ripe old age of 72. She was widowed again in 2000. When she was 92, she willingly gave up driving. Even though there were some hardships associated with this loss, all in all she had aged nicely in her modest one-story ranch house. She faced several health challenges during the last few years of her life: a rare form of anemia (MDA, mild dysplastic anemia) that required blood transfusions every 2-3 weeks; lymphoma at 94; and pneumonia later that same year. But she always found an inner strength that pulled her back from the slippery slope.

However, after her bout with pneumonia, she never fully recovered, and her vitality just was not what it used to be. The time had come when she needed support. Everyday tasks such as preparing meals had become too much for her, and she no longer could get in and out of the tub by herself (she did not take showers). I arranged for a home health aide to come three hours a day and I signed her up for Meals On Wheels (which came from the local state university and were exceptionally good and plentiful). Because she was in palliative care, she was eligible for a nurse and a home health aide from the VNA.

Introducing assistance gradually can be beneficial

Our parents often reject help, as it is an admission that they are no longer totally independent. Some have gotten used to living alone and feel that the presence of an aide is intrusive. However, aides can provide many types of services, and they do not have to come for long periods of time or seven days a week. For some parents, having an aide come for a couple of hours three days a week is all that is needed. Your parent may need help only at meal time, so you may arrange for an aide to come to make breakfast and dinner seven days a week. And even though there might be resistance initially, once the aides become familiar and a part of the routine, your parent may even look forward to their arrival. For me, knowing that an aide was coming to the house twice a day and that Meals On Wheels were also being delivered gave me peace of mind, as now several people were looking in on my mother during different times of day. Having aides come in for a limited amount of time can also serve as a test run to determine if this is the right agency for you. You will have a chance to evaluate if they are delivering the services you expect. Are they sending the type of person that you would like to take care of you? Are they compassionate and responsible?

If you are not satisfied, this is a great time to try another agency. Although I must confess that the type and quality of service needed during three hours a day versus 24/7 is different, nonetheless you hopefully will get a sense of the agency. You will at least have some idea how the director runs his or her company. Is there is adequate communication among the staff members? Do they arrive on time and complete their tasks? Or do they do as little as possible and just sit around and watch TV?

Meals On Wheels gets a bum rap

The image that Meals On Wheels conjures up is usually not a good one, as we typically visualize unappetizing canned peas, dried-out chicken, cold mashed potatoes, or overcooked meatballs in what was once spaghetti sauce. However, when it comes to Meals On Wheels, the quality can range from something practically inedible to something just this side of gourmet.

Fortunately for us, my mother's town was serviced by two different Meals On Wheels providers. One served the typical fare (not so appetizing), but the other provided food that was delicious and plentiful. Although it is unusual for two different providers to serve the same area, it is always a good idea to ask if there is more than one. You might also want to base your decision on the time of day the meals are delivered. Some services deliver midday meals, while others bring food in time for dinner. The meals are supposed to be nutritious, so you may want to check them out before you order them. The fee is quite nominal. My mother paid $4 a day.

Remember, however, that they are delivered only during the weekdays. Therefore, if your parent needs assistance with meals, you will have to make some other arrangements for the weekends.

Tips on managing the food in the refrigerator

Because the Meals On Wheels provider was part of the University of Massachusetts food service, the amount of food was often far more than my mother could possible eat (the servings must have been based on the appetites of male college students). The CNAs labeled the food as it arrived so they knew which containers needed to be thrown out according to their dates. We used standard labels that can be purchased at any office supply store.

On May 28, 2006, my mother celebrated her 95th birthday in style — with a lawn party and 50 guests, a big white tent, balloons, champagne, the works — she was the belle of the ball. Three weeks later, her life as she knew it came to a screeching halt after she fell and fractured her pelvis. Not being amenable to having Lifeline (I had it installed, and she had it removed), and not having her cell phone with her, she had to drag herself from the living room to the kitchen only to realize that she could not reach the phone. She then had to drag herself to her bedroom, which was on the other side of the house. She ended up knocking everything off her night table until she found the phone. She was in agony. And in addition to the excruciating pain from her fractured pelvis, her elbows were now bleeding. Her pelvis was fractured in two places, and she suffered multiple minor fractures.

The Lifeline "hang-up"

If your elderly parent lives alone, she really must have a Lifeline-like service or carry a cell phone. The disadvantage of a cell phone is that your parent must remember to keep it charged, turn it on, and learn how to use it. And it must be carried at all times. My mother insisted that if she had Lifeline, it would be a constant reminder that she might fall. I never quite understood her reasoning.

In addition to the familiar system requiring the user to wear a call button around the neck or wrist, various other high-tech passive monitoring devices are available that are far superior to the older Lifeline-type systems. Some of the newer monitoring devices include infrared and motion detector sensors placed in critical places such as the bedroom, bathroom, medicine cabinet, kitchen, front door, etc. They monitor the activity and establish a pattern that is normal for your parent. For example, if your mom normally spends 20 minutes in the bathroom in the morning but on a particular morning after 35 minutes she has not emerged, the wireless motion detector will transmit the data to a computer server. Caregivers can log on to the server, or the system can be set up to alert them or others on the call list by phone or by e-mail. More and more companies are providing this service. ADT's program called QuietCare offers this type of monitoring. Unlike video cameras, these sensors are not intrusive.

After making several calls, my mother finally reached a neighbor who called an ambulance. My mother was taken to the emergency room where her blood pressure was 54/32. The fact that she survived such a low blood pressure is a miracle. Typically, a pelvic fracture by itself is not the cause of death in the elderly, but the ensuing complications such as internal bleeding, infection, and an erratic blood pressure and heart rate can simply be too much for an aging body to cope with.

After this traumatic event, we were told to put my mother into hospice and bring her home so she could die in her own bed.

What to do if you cannot be there during your parent's hospitalization

During my mother's hospital stay, because she had become so paranoid from the Haldol and Ativan and thought everyone was trying to kill her, my nephew and I did 12-hour shifts. This also gave us an opportunity to monitor her care. If you cannot be with your parent during hospitalization, be sure you talk with the nurse and attending physician at least once a day. If neighbors and friends can visit regularly, they can be your eyes and ears as well. If not, you may want to consider hiring a private-duty nurse or CNA if you can afford it. Also, if you have siblings, decide among yourselves who the contact person should be so that everyone is not calling the nurses' station. Most hospitals are understaffed, and they do not have time to repeat the same information to each family member.

Coming home to die — or maybe not

We brought my mother home, as she had always wanted to die in her own bed. A new chapter was about to begin, in her life and in mine.

First of all, not all hospices are alike. The hospice assigned to care for my mother was a far cry from what hospice was like when my stepfather died in 2000. The staff's attitude and unwillingness to provide what seemed to me to be routine hospice care was a rude awakening for me. If you are unhappy with your hospice, check to see if there is another one in the area. I had no idea there was more than one hospice to choose from, nor did I know you could switch services. Later on during my mother's journey, I learned that some hospices are in a better position to provide the type of service that was par for the course a few years ago. If there is more than one hospice in your area, find out which one is actively fundraising, as that may determine the quality of service.

Second, not all in-home 24/7 CNA providers offer the same caliber aides or the same level of care. The first agency we hired (which I refer to agency number 1) was extremely expensive and required that a family member be the case manager. In my mother's case, I took on this role. Because home health care agencies are licensed by the state, the scope of what CNAs could provide was quite limited. In fact, it was rather shocking to discover what they could and could not do. Navigating the medical system from there on out was an amazing experience.

The first hurdle, believe it or not, was to get hospice to cooperate. After my mother was discharged, her arrival at the house was delayed, so the hospice nurse was told not to come. However, this nurse was in charge of developing my mother's medical care plan, a plan that the CNAs needed to provide care. Arriving with a boatload of medications, we needed a medical plan that day — tomorrow wouldn't do. After all, my mother was critically ill and had come home to die, and I had CNAs at the house who needed a medical plan before they could do their job. After 15 or 20 minutes of negotiating with hospice, I finally got them to agree to send the hospice nurse to the house that evening.

During this conversation with hospice, I asked them, "What exactly do you provide?" They told me about their counseling services, which we were not interested in. I was more concerned about their medical services, which in the case of this particular hospice were so minimal that it was almost frightening. The day my mother came home from the hospital, we received the typical comfort pack, which contained meds that my mom didn't tolerate. Morphine made her throw up, and Ativan and Haldol had caused her to hallucinate and become paranoid. Those were the drugs in the comfort pack. I asked that we be sent alternative drugs, but that never happened.

When I inquired about what they would do if my mother experienced respiratory distress while she was actively dying, they told me I could call them and that they would walk me through what I needed to do. And if that did not work, I could call 911. Well, thanks a lot for nothing. In 2000, when my stepfather died at home, the hospice nurse was there for several hours two to three days a week and on call 24/7 and would come if you called her. Here someone was on call but would only provide phone support. So not only was I going to be on my own, but also I had a comfort pack full of meds I could not administer. Quite frankly, I was terrified — would I be able to handle my mother's passing by myself?

What may surprise you

There may be more than one hospice organization serving your area, and you can change providers. If you feel your parent's or your needs are not being met, do not hesitate to see if another hospice provider may be able to step in. I had no idea that this was an option. When my mother entered hospice a second time, after she was discharged from rehab following her "miraculous" recovery, we signed up with another organization that provided a level of care reminiscent of what it was like when my stepfather died.

Before signing up with a particular hospice, it might be useful to check to see if they are actively fundraising. The problem with many programs is that they have suffered severe budget cuts. However, some programs pursue grants and other monies and are therefore in a better position to provide more comprehensive services.

In-home care: CNA services from agency number 1 — the good, the bad and the ugly

Although I am grateful that we were in a financial position to afford CNA care for my mother, let me explain the pitfalls that can be associated with this kind of service. The first agency (agency number 1) provided no consistency. We never received a schedule, so we never knew who was going to arrive for which shift, and every time there was a new person (something that happened with great frequency), someone had to show them where everything was. Theoretically, the person whose shift ended was expected to bring the new arrival up to speed about what had transpired during the last eight hours and what the needs were for the next eight hours. Because so many of the CNAs arrived 15-30 minutes late, the transferring of information often didn't happen. This kind of "care" can only work if a family member is on site around the clock.

The importance of consistency

If there is a core group of CNAs assigned to care for your parent, they get to know your parent and the routine. More importantly, your parent does not have to deal with new people all the time. Change is hard for the elderly. Even when the CNA is not great, sometimes your parent will prefer that person to having to get to know someone new. Make sure your agency provides you with a schedule.

Knowing who is coming ahead of time will help quell your parent's anxiety, and she may even look forward to the arrival of a particular CNA. My mother clearly bonded with some of the CNAs and looked forward to seeing them.

Keeping a consistent team in place is even more important for patients with Alzheimer's and for patients nearing the end of their lives.

It is very distressing for people with Alzheimer's to have any change — the tighter the routine and the greater the familiarity, the better. For some patients who are actively dying, anxiety levels are heightened at this stage, and seeing new faces can be unnecessarily stressful. If possible, ask the agency to send CNAs who have worked the greatest number of hours, as those are the ones who can offer the greatest comfort during a parent's last days. Even though friends and caregivers are well intentioned, unless they are very close to your parent, you should discourage them from coming at this time. For example, my mother's financial planner wanted to say good-bye, but my mother had only seen her a few times in her life and had not seen her in at least a year. It was hard to tell her not to come, but I thought that was in my mother's best interest.

Because my mother was on fentanyl and Dilaudid®, narcotic painkillers, she had a lot of trouble with her bowels. If I had not inquired daily as to the status, the meds needed to help regulate her would not have been administered.

The model of having three CNAs a day (versus one provider who provides 24-hour care, which has its own benefits as well as drawbacks) can result in a lack of consistency in the patient's care. Because there really is not a case manager on site, this system can easily fall apart unless a family member steps in and takes on the role of case manager or, as I have called it, the role of parent care coordinator. However, I did learn that if you hire a competent agency, in-home care can run quite smoothly and independently, provided that there has been enough staff orientation and the lines of communication are open and active between all parties.

CNAs do not earn a lot of money. They are young or not-so-young women. Some may not have finished high school, while others may be part-time college students or nursing students. Many are single moms who are barely getting by. They have the demands of child care and child rearing and often have ex-husbands who are unavailable. Some of these young moms are simply overwhelmed with the stresses of life. So if her relief is late and the CNA must pick up her kids from day care, the transfer of patient information can get dropped in the shuffle as one CNA arrives and the other dashes out the door. However, this is not always the case, as many CNAs are very dedicated to their profession. And, once in a while, there is a gem who goes beyond the call of duty.

How do agency owners treat their staff?

The two agencies we worked with clearly embraced two very different cultures. It was clear that the attitudes and compassion from the people at the top filtered down to the staff. If the person in charge was compassionate and gave 110%, then that was reflected in the staff.

Agency number 1 made sure that none of their staff worked more than 30 hours a week so the agency did not have to pay benefits. As a result, many of their staff were discontented. When staff are not well compensated for their work and are not respected by their bosses, it is only natural that this dissatisfaction is reflected in the type of care delivered. It is hard to take pride in one's work under these conditions. Most of the aides from agency number 1 were stressed-out single moms struggling to make ends meet.

On the other hand, agency number 2 not only had full-time staff who worked 40 hours a week and received benefits, but also allowed them to work overtime, for which they were paid time-and-a-half. The aides from agency number 2 were either single or married with children, and some were nursing students. Having husbands at home to help with child care made it easier for the aides to log in 40+ hours a week. Given that the quality of care can be affected by the level of compensation and respect that the aides are given by their superiors, it might be beneficial to ask an agency about their hiring policy and how their aides are compensated.

Be clear as to what CNAs can and cannot do

In Massachusetts, health care agencies are certified by the state, and CNAs are not allowed to administer any meds from prescription bottles, mix over-the-counter (OTC) meds like MiraLax®, administer suppositories, or even cut a section out of a DuoDERM® patch and place it on the skin to prevent a bedsore. They cannot perform any function that resembles treatment of any kind. They cannot take Tylenol® out of a Tylenol bottle. They can only take meds out of a pillbox. So for someone like my mom who was actively dying, prescriptions given as needed (PRN), such as nitroglycerin, or OTC meds had to be handled by a family member.

Certification of home health care agencies

Each state has its own certification procedures, requirements, and laws. However, depending on the state, some home health care agencies may be certified, whereas others may operate without licenses or certification. Part of your research should include which governing agencies have the authority to certify home health care agencies in your state. When you are in the process of selecting an agency, make sure you ask about their certification status.

So what can CNAs do? They can take pills out of a med box that has been filled by a family member, a nurse from hospice, the VNA, or the agency, and give it to the patient. They can help with bathing or give sponge baths, apply lotions to the skin, clean patients up, prepare meals, go grocery shopping, run errands, or do light housekeeping (although the willingness to do this varies from person to person). Some are great and will clean up the kitchen and do laundry, while others prefer to sit and do as little as possible.

What is the best kind of pillbox to buy?

I found that a pillbox with four different compartments for each day of the week worked best. The times may not coincide with what your parent needs, but you can just cover them up with a label listing the correct times. This type of pillbox seems to eliminate mistakes and confusion. They can be purchased at any place that carries pharmaceuticals and medical supplies or on the Internet.

There are also all sorts of high-tech pillboxes with alarms and sensors. MedSignals and the MD.2 Personal Medication System, which give verbal and text alerts, automatically dispense pills and monitor missed doses. These may be useful if your parent is receiving just a few hours of CNA support or for a parent who is still living alone and independently. MIT and the Rhode Island School of Design have even developed a soft and fuzzy Electronic Pill Pet that uses play and emotion to remind older adults to take their medications.

Hospice care versus palliative care

Prior to my mother's fall, she was in palliative care because she had a rare form of anemia and the treatments she had been taking in addition to transfusions were no longer working. As a palliative care patient, she was eligible for services provided by the VNA. Once a week the VNA nurse came to take her vitals, and a home health aide came twice weekly to bathe her. If a patient is in hospice care, a hospice nurse and aide are available. One big difference between palliative care and hospice is that hospice pays for certain items like renting a hospital bed, an over-the-bed tray, a walker, oxygen, meds, etc. However, while in hospice a patient cannot receive treatment other than that which will keep them comfortable. This restriction is being revisited in some states, as it is more cost-effective to have people in hospice than in hospitals.

As my mother began to rally, we needed to know if this was the high before the final decline, or if she was really getting better. One vital piece of information was to know what her hematocrit was, as this would be a strong indicator of her current level of health and potential for further improvement. However, blood tests are not allowed by hospice, so we had to take her out of hospice and place her back into palliative care. The lab work confirmed that she was getting better. The next step was to place her into rehab where she could get the medical care she needed.

Palliative care versus in-home hospice care

Palliative care is for patients who are no longer benefiting from lifesaving treatment but may have a longer time to live than the 6-month cap placed on hospice patients. Services available include a visiting nurse who typically comes once a week, a home health aide that helps with bathing usually two or three times a week, a physical therapist who comes once or twice a week, and a social worker. Usually, the patient is still treated by a physician and continues to go to medical appointments.

Hospice is a comprehensive regimen of care that provides support to family members and care to patients facing an end-of-life illness. Hospice focuses on the quality of life as they strive to make the dying patient as comfortable as possible. Patients eligible for hospice care usually have no more than six months to live. At this stage, patients no longer receive treatment. Instead, comfort care is provided by a hospice nurse and a home health aide as well as hospice volunteers. Because the nature of dying is so individual, no one can predict what course will be followed. The goal of the hospice team is to be sensitive and responsive to the special needs of each individual and to family members.

The frequency of visits is based on need. As patients become more frail, the number of visits increase. Through Medicare, hospice also pays for medical equipment and medications related to the patient's hospice diagnosis. As mentioned earlier, the parameters for hospice care are evolving, so you may want to call your local hospital to see what is available in your area. (Note: Some residential hospices are loosening their requirements and are accepting patients who may live longer than six months and who have chosen to continue with their treatment regimens.)

Information about hospice is available from your local hospital, your state hospice organizations, or the National Hospice Helpline (800-658-8898), as well as from the National Council of Hospice Professionals Physician Section. You can also find information about hospice from the American Cancer Society, the American Association of Retired Persons (AARP), and the Social Security Administration.

Rehab — what to look for when selecting a facility

Frequently, when a patient is discharged from the hospital to a rehab facility, placement depends on the availability of a bed at the time of discharge or on the financial resources of the individual. I was fortunate in that my mother and I were able to make the decisions about where she was to go.

While my mother was in the hospital, prior to her developing life-threatening complications, she was expected to go directly from the hospital into rehab. Not being familiar with the area, I checked out several facilities. A number of factors needed to be considered, such as keeping our search within a certain radius of the hospital and within the jurisdiction of her physician. We also wanted to make sure that the facility was within a reasonable distance from friends and neighbors so they could visit her as often as possible.

In addition, certain things were very important to my mother. Some may seem superficial, but they would dictate whether she would be able to tolerate being in a rehab facility. For example, the environment needed to be upscale and somewhat cheerful. She was a very picky eater, so the food had to be better than canned vegetables and macaroni and cheese. The patient population needed to be more rehab-oriented and not mentally challenged. She would not have done well with a mixed population including patients with dementia or recovering from a stroke. We also wanted a location convenient to the hospital where she received her transfusions, as she had a fractured pelvis and sitting was very difficult and painful. One of the factors that I felt was of critical importance was the PT room, that is, how well equipped it was, the ambiance, and the level of experience of the therapists.

Factors to consider when selecting a rehab facility:

- Staffing ratios
- Staff turnover
- Number of CNAs per shift
- Experience of PTs and OTs
- Is the staff on contract or do they work full-time for the facility

- Size of the PT room and type of equipment
- Types of patients (are they cognizant rehab patients or is there a mixed population including patients with dementia or patients recovering from a stroke)
- Food
- Smells (good smells or bad smells)
- Cleanliness
- Tidiness
- In-house laundry facility
- In-house hairdresser
- Convenience to doctors and hospitals
- Convenience for friends and family to visit.

Some older facilities that have not been renovated often have phone jacks and cable access, but the patient must supply her own phone and TV. This might be an issue for, some. Because you already have to bring clothes, shoes slippers, toiletries, and whatever items you feel might personalize your parent's room, having to bring a TV and phone just adds to the list and increases the number of trips you have to make.

Depending on your parent's needs you may want to ask if they supply headphones, so that your parent is not disturbed by her roommate and vice versa. (For information on how to select a rehab facility, see pages 186-195.)

Of the four facilities I looked at, the one in which my mother was placed met all of the criteria. They had the best food, and although it was still somewhat institutionalized, at least it wasn't chicken nuggets, sloppy joes, macaroni and cheese, and canned vegetables. They served fresh fruit and salads, and a selection of various proteins ranging from cottage cheese and yogurt to chicken, tuna fish, veal, etc. Most places have just one choice.

The PT room was quite large, with lots of equipment. In one of the facilities I visited, the PT room was tiny, and half of it was being used for storing chairs. In my mother's rehab facility, staff could work with four to five patients at a time. Patients got to know each other and could offer each other moral support — a rather nice concept.

However, her facility fell short on having enough staff, CNAs in particular. This is not an uncommon problem. I had to supplement her CNA care with two hours a day of private care in the morning so that she could get bathed and dressed in a timely fashion. If providing private care is something you are interested in doing, check into this ahead of time, as some nursing homes and rehab facilities will not allow the hiring of private CNAs.

The shortage of CNAs is ubiquitous

If you have the money, supplementing CNA care, at least during the 7:00 am-3:00 pm shift, can be invaluable. CNAs are stretched thinnest during the morning shift, as they have to bathe and dress everyone and serve breakfast and lunch. None of the facilities I visited had adequate staffing. One facility I heard about was going to have to bathe four people before the 7:00 am shift, which meant patients would be showered at 5:00, 5:30, 6:00, and 6:30 am. I personally would not appreciate being awakened at 5:00 am for a shower!

> Because of the staff shortage during the morning shift, I hired a private CNA for 2 hours each morning, who bathed and dressed my mother; otherwise she would have had to wait several hours, which was unacceptable to her. However, some nursing homes will not allow private CNAs, so if you want to provide this added care, check with the nursing home prior to placing your parent.

When my mother first arrived at the rehab facility, she did not want to stay. She hated the place. I stayed a few extra days in Massachusetts to help her make the transition before going back home to North Carolina. She was clearly unhappy, but if she wanted to regain any quality of life, she had to be in rehab. When she arrived, she was so debilitated that she could not even reposition herself in bed. She was going to have to get stronger to be able to go back home.

She was in a double room on the window side, but because she had a roommate who kept her curtain drawn all the time, my mother was cut off from her roommate and all the activity taking place outside her door. My mother was a people person and loved to talk, and this roommate was basically non-communicative. Even when my cousin visited with his three Yorkshire Terriers (yes, dogs were welcomed), my mother's roommate did not show any signs of acknowledging the dogs or my cousin or his wife. Nor did she engage in any conversation with any of the many other visitors. She had been there for months and had a reputation of being an extremely sullen, unhappy person.

> **What to do if the rehab facility you have chosen does not work out**
>
> Hopefully you had a chance to do your research ahead of time, and you are familiar with other options. And even if you did visit some other facilities, it is always a good idea to ask for recommendations. Time is of the essence. Most elderly patients do not deal well with change, and they may even prefer staying in an inferior place once they have acclimated to their environment and have gotten to know some of the staff. Therefore, if you have uncovered problems that cannot be resolved, the sooner your parent can be transferred to another facility, the better.

A new government-sponsored 5-star rating system of nursing homes, similar to the one used for hotels, is now available. These federal regulations will require all nursing homes to have a sprinkler system in place by 2013. Currently only one out of every 11 nursing homes has a sprinkler system — and there are about 16,000 nursing homes in the United States. Another industry trade group, the American health care Association, has determined that the new ranking system should not depend solely on data obtained during inspections, but should also include levels of satisfaction of both consumers and staff.

Understanding medications

Over the past 12 years, I have worked as medical writer and have written about dozens and dozens of pharmaceuticals. I am therefore very familiar with and comfortable reading the Physician's Desk Reference (PDR) — a must for anyone who is trying to manage the health care of a loved one. In the PDR you can look up prescription medications and read about side effects, dosing, and drug interactions, etc. You can also find this information on the Internet by Googling the name of the drug followed by "package insert" (PI). Whenever your parent is prescribed a new medication, it is always a good idea to know what kinds of side effects are possible. This information is useful if all of a sudden your parent complains about a new symptom possibly associated with the medication. Sometimes a substitute medication will be as effective but will not have the same side effects. For example, your parent may not do well on Nexium®, so she may be given Prevacid® instead.

Before my mother was ever given a new medication, I investigated it thoroughly to explore the potential side effects. For example, if a medication was recommended that had side effects mimicking an existing condition, such as edema, how would it be possible to know if her congestive heart failure or the drug was causing the edema? In these instances, I requested that another drug be substituted or that she simply not take the new medication.

If your parent complains of new symptoms, talk with her physicians, as she may be experiencing side effects from a particular medication or from a drug-drug interaction.

Keeping track of your parent's medications is critical

A crucial piece in managing your parent's health and ensuring that she enjoys a good quality of life is to make sure that she is taking her medications and that there is no confusion. Understanding what she is taking and how new meds might interact with her current regimen are also very important.

If she is experiencing side effects, you can discuss this the next time you are at a doctor's appointment or when you are picking up a prescription at the pharmacy. Pharmacists are very knowledgeable about side effects and drug-drug interactions. If your parent is not cognitively impaired and does not have significant memory problems, encourage her to communicate her side effects directly with her physician, even if you accompany her to the appointment.

Even before your parent needs assistance, make a list with her of the medications she takes and check the expiration dates. When you make the list, be sure to list the brand name and the generic name to avoid any confusion. This will be particularly useful if your parent is seeing more than one doctor. (For example, Tylenol is the brand name and acetaminophen is the generic name. See Sample Prescription Medications Log in Appendix B.) Give your parent a copy and keep one for yourself.

Buy yourself a copy of the Physician's Desk Reference, or learn to search medications and their side effects on the Internet by Googling the name of the drug followed by "PI" (for example, Lipitor® PI or Lipitor package insert). Scroll down to the section that lists side effects. If you do not have the time or if you feel uncomfortable doing this, then hire someone to do it for you. (See section on geriatric care managers, page 157.)

During the first couple of weeks my mother was in rehab, I noticed on several occasions that her speech was slurred. She sounded as if she were drunk or drugged. I asked the nurse if she had been given anything new and was told that she had not. I asked my mother about her pain level, a question that amazingly was never put to her by the staff or even by the PT. My mom told me she did not have any pain. I suspected that her slurred speech was directly related to her pain patch. Because she was on a 75 mcg fentanyl patch, I asked if she could be titrated off (a process that steps down the dose). Of course, this request had to be given to her doctor, who could then write an order for the titration. If I had not made this request, it is anyone's guess how long she would have been kept on this medication. When I inquired why the doctor had not initiated the reduction in her pain meds, I was told that this is often overlooked — another broken piece in our health care system.

There were several reasons to get her off the patch: 1) like all opioids, it caused severe constipation; 2) it caused her mouth to be so dry that she had major swallowing issues and had to have all of her food pureed, making it so unappealing that she would not eat it; 3) it caused her to be very hot (prior to her fall she was always extremely cold); and 4) she exhibited confusion, which was a new symptom, as my mother had always been clear-headed prior to the fall. I actually was not sure if the confusion was perhaps a result of her fall or a side effect of the medication.

Within a couple of days of starting the titration process, her speech became less slurred and she no longer was confused. Her swallowing status improved slowly as her mouth started to secrete more saliva. Once she was weaned completely off the patch, she was no longer hot and went back to being cold.

> **Don't be afraid to be assertive and to ask questions**
>
> If you are concerned about the side effects of a particular drug, talk to the medical staff or to your parent's primary care physician. I am certain if I had not initiated the titration of my mother's fentanyl patch, she would have been on it for many more weeks than was necessary.

When things go terribly wrong

After my mom had been in rehab for a couple of weeks, I started to receive phone calls from friends concerning my mother's care. This is every adult child's worst nightmare. Did I put my mother in a facility where she was being ignored or, even worse, abused? In three days I received three unsolicited phone calls from three different visitors. The story was the same: my mother had been soiled for an hour and a half before being changed. The third call was the most upsetting. Not only had she waited to be cleaned, but she had also missed PT because of the delay. And when the staff came to clean her, they were angry and rough enough with her that my mom's neighbor told me, "It was horrible to watch." My God, what had I done? I thought I had selected the best facility.

My fingers could not dial the number of the facility fast enough. After I left multiple messages for the director of the facility, the directors of nursing and PT/OT, and the charge nurse, they called back on a conference call. I once had a colleague who used to say she was so angry she could spit nails. Now I was at that point myself. I went ballistic. Not being changed in a timely manner (within 10-15 minutes) can result in skin breakdown. For an elderly person with extremely thin skin and a very low platelet count, any bedsore can mean death. The directors made all sorts of promises and even moved my mother to a private room directly across from the nurses' station. The move was intended to help reduce response time and also to give my mother a break from her asocial roommate. Unfortunately, the problem was not where my mother was placed, but the fact that they simply did not have enough staff.

The more visitors your parent has, the better

If your parent is in a facility or at home in another state with no family members nearby, make sure someone (a friend or neighbor) is willing to check in on her. If there is no one who can visit, hire an advocate such as a Geriatric Care Manager or contact your local ombudsman. You must have an unbiased person drop by to assess whether the services that you are expecting are actually being delivered and that your parent is being well taken care of.

Some of the things to look for: Is your parent well kempt? Is her hair combed? Is she clean and wearing clean clothes? Is her room neat and tidy? Is it free of odors and smells? Does she seem stressed out, or does she talk cheerfully with the staff? Is she maintaining her weight, or does she look considerably thinner? Is she attending PT and OT regularly?

After assurances from all parties that it would not happen again, the next day, while in her private room across from the nurses' station, my mother waited almost two hours to be changed! I had already called the ombudsman. I now needed to get on a plane as soon as possible.

Yes, the squeaky wheel does get the grease, but at what price? Some staff were sympathetic; others became even more belligerent and less cooperative.

When I arrived, I expressed my gratitude to many of the staff for the care they were providing my mother. I knew that what caused the lack of response was not so much an attitude problem but simply the lack of warm bodies. As a matter of fact, my mother hated to use her call button, because she could see how the CNAs were not walking, but running, from room to room. And bless her heart, she felt sorry for them.

Being short-staffed is something that plagues all nursing homes and rehab facilities. CNAs are in such demand that if they are unhappy at one facility, they can just quit and go somewhere else. Unless CNAs are paid higher wages, this staff shortage will probably get worse before it gets better.

Despite the various hurdles, my mom made a lot of progress. However, she decided that she no longer wanted to continue with her transfusions, so in spite of having learned to walk with a walker and having conquered her incontinence, she decided to transition to in-home hospice, in-home care, and Lifeline. Although she resisted having Lifeline, it was a condition of her discharge, as she was home for eight hours each day without a CNA.

Home at Last

She is frail. She is 95.
Bright yellow pee fills her catheter bag
Incontinence, a by-product of a fractured pelvis.

Harsh fluorescent lights cast a ghostly hue
Making her pale skin even paler
Her body ravaged by anemia.

Seven long weeks of PT and OT
she walks ever so slowly
aided by her walker.

Once taken for granted,
she now savors the little joys of life.
Her own bed. Ah, to sleep when sleep beckons.
Sweet slumber. No more 6:00 AM wakeup calls.
She "orders" what she wants to eat.
What a luxury, an indulgence.
Her aide brings her a slice of tiramisu.

Compassionate providers care for her.
At your service, madam.
They touch her gently and massage her worn-out body.
The room is filled with the scent of lavender.
They paint her nails and make her look beautiful,

recapturing a hint of her aristocratic past.
She was always the epitome of elegance.

No more waiting and waiting,
Sitting in soiled diapers.
No more ringing and ringing the bell
that falls on deaf ears.
No more accidents.
She lives out her days
with dignity, respect, and grace.

Monitoring devices can help reduce CNA costs

Unless your parent is bedridden or has advanced Alzheimer's disease or dementia, it might be possible for her to spend several hours a day alone. If this is the case, systems like Lifeline or a passive monitoring system can help keep her safe. The amount of time and times of day she can be home alone should be determined by the medical staff.

Given the high hourly rates of CNAs, using Lifeline or a system like QuietCare can result in substantial savings. Using the national average of $19/hour for a CNA, having only 16 hours of care per day versus 24 hours will save you over $1,000 a week and over $4,000 a month.

Cost-$aving Tips when hiring CNAs

16 Hours/Day	Round-the-Clock Care	Savings
16 hrs/day x 7 days x $19/hr = $2,128/week or $9,120/month	24 hrs x 7 days x $19/hr = $3,192/ week or $13,680/ month	$1,064/week or $4,560/month

In our case, 16 hours/day at $18.50 cost $2,072/ week or $8,288/month versus round-the-clock care for $3,108/week or $12,432/month. As my mother became weaker and eventually was bedridden, we increased the CNA hours to 24/7. If your parent is in hospice, the hospice home health aide can fill in some of the hours not covered by the home health care agency.

How CNA services can and should be delivered: Doing it the right way with agency number 2

Communication is key

Before my mother was discharged from rehab, I lost sleep pondering how she would be able to come home and live in the care of CNAs. If I was not going to live in her house, who was going to fill the role of case manager?

The last agency we hired was totally incapable of providing unsupervised care or managing her treatment plan. With a bit of perseverance and luck, I was able to find an agency that provided superior service. I actually had contacted this agency two other times, but they were too busy to help us out. But as they say, the third time is a charm. The owner of this agency, a nurse, was committed to making sure that her patients received the help they needed. Her staff seemed to be better educated, as she offered them in-service training and made sure they were up to speed on the particular needs of each patient. She wrote out specific care plans for each shift, and the staff had to initial that each aspect of the care plan was fulfilled (see Appendix B). In my mother's case, because of her constant battle with constipation, a special sheet was designed to keep track of her bowel movements. A treatment plan in the form of a flow-chart was created to offer first-, second-, and third-line treatment for her constipation.

My mother was also prone to experiencing distressing events such as anxiety, pressure in her chest, nausea, stomach pain, and shortness of breath. Therefore, we designed flow charts for each of these potential problems. Because I am a medical writer, I am used to writing algorithms — a medical term for flow charts. But they really are quite simple. They do not have to be fancy. They basically describe the problem, outline the criteria that should be followed, and what should be tried first. In case of nausea, the first line of treatment might be something as simple as saltine crackers or ginger ale. If that does not work, perhaps Maalox® or a cup of ginger tea would help. Anyway, you get the idea.

> ### The key to seamless in-home health care services is having a good communications system in place
>
> Good communication should include 1) the ability of the staff to get in touch with their supervisor at all times, 2) following schedules and flowcharts, and 3) keeping an accurate log so that all staff are literally and figuratively on the same page. If there is a change in status, staff should know to notify the supervisor or the hospice nurse, who are both available around the clock. By nipping a potential problem in the bud, the likelihood of something small becoming something big is diminished.

> For example, if there is redness on the skin and it looks worrisome, calling the nurse on call could prevent the red patch from becoming a pressure sore.

Agency number 2 always provided us with a schedule for two weeks to one month at a time. That way, my mother knew whom to expect, which helped reduce her anxiety. She kept the schedule by her side, and at times it provided her with a little joy if she knew that one of the CNAs with whom she had developed a special bond was scheduled to come. It actually gave her something to look forward to.

Because the staff of this new agency reported to the director daily, if there was an issue it was addressed right away.

> **Make sure that wherever the CNAs are in the house, they can hear your parent**
>
> Baby monitors are invaluable in keeping tabs on a parent who spends most of her time in bed but needs assistance with toileting. If your parent's house is small, one baby monitor will suffice. At night, depending on which room the CNA is using, it is advisable to have the baby monitor right next to her. Then if she should happen to doze off (which she is allowed to do — she is not allowed to fall into a deep sleep), she will still wake up to the rustling sounds from the monitor. Individuals who need assistance with toileting are more likely to fall at night when they are half asleep, so it is critical that the CNA assist them. The MALEM Enuresis Wireless Remote Bed Alarm signals an alarm when your parent gets up from the bed (see page 61).

If you find that the CNA does not hear your parent over the monitor, having a chime that your parent can ding or a bell she can ring will get the CNA's attention. My mother used an energy chime (designed more for meditators) that had three different tones. One was so high-pitched that it would have been impossible to sleep through it.

The importance of CNA orientation

When new CNAs are assigned, they should first be oriented by the staff before providing services. New CNAs should arrive during another CNA's shift, and this person should show them where the meds and the med box are kept, which creams to use after bathing, where nightgowns and underwear are located, the location of laundry supplies, where different food is stored, etc. CNAs should also go over the log book and specific instructions. This orientation is at the expense of the client but is well worth it. During this time, the new aides learn the ropes and are introduced to your parent.

Because change is difficult for the elderly, being introduced to new staff members prior to the start of a shift is a brilliant idea

This is particularly true for staff who work the night shift, as the elderly can be a bit more confused or disoriented at night. By meeting the person during orientation, the surprise factor of waking up in the middle of the night and being greeted by a total stranger is avoided.

(Seeing strange faces in the night, something she experienced with agency number 1, was very disorienting and disconcerting for my mother.)

What might be obvious to you may be a challenge for the CNAs

Many CNAs are from other countries. If they are young and have not been in the United States for a long time, some appliances (like washing machines, dryers, or dishwashers) can be a bit challenging for them. If your appliances are high-tech, be sure to go over the operating instructions.

Although we know that dish soap cannot be used in a dishwasher, it is totally logical to think that it can. After all, dishes are dishes and soap is soap. One of the CNAs from Lesotho drew this erroneous conclusion and put liquid dish soap in the dishwasher. The result was not catastrophic, but suds were everywhere, oozing out of the dishwasher and onto the floor. It was as if we had just stumbled into an *I Love Lucy* episode.

Washers, dryers, dishwashers, and stoves are becoming more and more high-tech each year. Some have numerous electronic buttons and reset buttons. What we think is common knowledge is not necessarily so. Therefore take the time to make sure that everyone knows how to use and maintain your appliances.

Another maintenance issue is cleaning the filter in the dryer. During one of my visits to see my mother, I thought I should check the dryer, and I discovered that the filter was loaded with lint. As you know, this can be a fire hazard. I had asked the aide to do this, but she had looked only under the dryer for the filter, as this is where it is located in dryers in her country.

> On another visit, the electricity went out in part of the house. An electrical spike had caused the circuit breaker to switch off, and as a result, most of the house was in the dark. Be sure that your CNAs know where the circuit breaker box is located and are shown how to turn the electricity back on. Be sure that a flashlight is kept in a convenient spot, and that everyone knows where it is. It seems that these events always happen at night. Also make sure that caregivers know when trash day is and what gets recycled when.

After my mother came home and agency number 2 was on board, I spent another five days at her home so that I could observe the staff and answer their questions. I made it a point to get to know the staff who were taking care of my mother. I spent time with each of the CNAs so that I could learn a little about their lives and make at least a superficial connection with them before I headed back home. I needed to get a feeling for who they were. If I were in need of care, would I feel comfortable with them? Were they cheerful and happy to help, or were they feeling a bit put out? I also needed to assess whether they would be able to carry on without me. Would the system we had carefully put into place work without a family member living in the house? I am pleased to report that the aides were great and that our system worked like a well-oiled machine.

Two of the main differences between this agency and the previous one were the caliber of staff and an enhanced communication system. The staff were better compensated by agency number 2, and they had a much more detailed log book that prompted them to do certain things. Everything was recorded in addition to writing notes. (See Appendix B for sample flow charts and schedules) There also was a nurse on call 24/7. This was critical, as CNAs do not have a lot of training. If the client's status changed, or if the client was experiencing pain or nausea or had become belligerent (as clients with Alzheimer's sometimes do), the CNAs could call someone to get advice. Not all agencies provide this kind of support to their CNAs, so this is something that deserves to be investigated prior to signing a contract.

> Make sure that the home health agency you hire provides a nurse on call around the clock.

Sometimes it is the little things that count

It is important to honor how your parent lived her life. For example, my mother was someone who was always dressed to the nines and always wore skirts and high heels (until she developed some balance issues), jewelry, and makeup. When she went to rehab and needed to wear slacks, I had to buy her a new wardrobe, as she did not own any slacks or shorts. And true to form, on the day she went to rehab in an ambulance and was on oxygen, she put on her lipstick and makeup. After all, how could she leave the house without looking her best?

After she left rehab and was in in-home hospice, it was important to her to still look attractive. Even as she grew weaker and weaker, if visitors came she would ask for her comb, pressed powder, and lipstick. Until she was 94, she did her own nails. She loved to have her nails manicured, so I went out and bought her nail polish that matched her lipstick. The aides enjoyed painting my mother's nails, and she loved the way her nails looked.

My mother was the epitome of femininity, and I made sure she had an ample supply of beautiful, feminine night-gowns. She hated anything that reminded her of the hospital and therefore would have hated to wear hospital johnnies.

As she declined and was no longer able to sit up on her own, I cut the backs of her nightgowns so they functioned more or less like hospital johnnies, but she still looked elegant. And even during her last days, when she was very weak and very ill, I made sure that she still looked beautiful, that she was clean, and that her gown was fresh and free from stains or spots.

Some men and women pride themselves on how they look. They love to look dashing or beautiful, they like to be well-coiffed and groomed, and they love to be clean and wear clean clothes. If your parent falls into this category, then honor that lifestyle. If your dad is ill or dying, make sure he is clean-shaven and his hair is combed, and maybe spritz him with his favorite aftershave or cologne. Let him wear his favorite pajamas; the tops will do, as the bed linens will take care of the rest.

If your mom is the one who is ill or dying, do whatever you can to help her look pretty and feel good about herself. When my mother was in the final stages of dying, the hospice nurse brought over a couple of hospital johnnies and commented that my mother would not have wanted to wear them. At the time, my mother was in a deep sleep and was unresponsive. I agreed and decided to destroy perfectly good nightgowns by cutting them up the back and dressing her in something she would have felt good in.

CHAPTER 4

What I Learned: Specific Suggestions

To move or not to move — moving closer to an adult child or staying at home with what is familiar

After my stepfather died, my mother and I discussed the possibility of her moving closer to me, but at the time of my stepfather's death, she was already 88 years old. And although she was still driving and was relatively healthy, the thought of having to leave what was familiar was simply overwhelming. Change is quite difficult for octogenarians and is even more challenging when they have to do it alone, without a spouse. My mother had had the same hairdresser for 25 years and the same doctor for many years, and she had her circle of friends and wonderful neighbors. The idea of leaving all that behind and starting anew was really quite daunting. It would have been difficult even for someone much younger.

The downside to aging at home

As our parents give up driving, they become prime candidates for becoming isolated and, consequently, depressed. This is particularly true for those who live out in the suburbs or in the country. Elderly parents who reside in more urban environments can still get out and about as long as they are able to walk independently.

If you do not have family members who live near your parent, then you may want to see if you can line up someone to drive her to doctors' appointments, take her shopping, or just take her on outings or rides. It is important for your parent to be able to get out of the house.

We all know how time speeds up as we get older, but it sort of goes into reverse mode for those who do not have much going on in their lives. The days can drag on, and the time between visits from family and friends can seem like an eternity. However, if there is a special event coming up, such as a family reunion or a birthday, it can give your parent something to look forward to.

Become familiar with your parent's community

If your parent is living in a city or town that you did not grow up in, then you will need to spend time becoming acquainted with the area. During your visits, make a point of getting to know your parent's friends and neighbors. You may want to invite them over for lunch or take them out. Accompany your parent to the bank and get to know the tellers and loan officers.

> Get to know her doctors, and go with her to appointments. Meeting her doctors face-to-face will serve you well when you need to call them on your parent's behalf. Make a list of names and phone numbers, and enter the important ones into your cell phone. Developing relationships with people who are key to your parent's life will prove invaluable when you find yourself having to take care of your parent from a distance.
>
> Be sure that one or more neighbors has a key to the house so that if you should call and there is no answer, you can call these neighbors to check on your parent. It is extremely anxiety-provoking to call for several hours not knowing if your parent is all right.

Troubleshooting before there is trouble

When planning care for a loved one, one must think of all the "what-ifs." So before I hired the second agency, I made a list.

The first set of what-ifs had to do with my mother's care. What if my mother has chest pain — what would be the first line of treatment? I asked similar questions for other possible episodes like nausea, anxiety, constipation, etc. What if staff get sick and cannot come — who will fill in? What if there is a snow or ice storm, and the roads are too hazardous? What if there is a power outage, and there is no heat for several days? What is the contingency plan?

The answer to "What if an aide gets sick or has a family emergency and cannot report to work," was that a substitute would be called to fill in. If there was a delay, the owner of the company, a nurse, would stay with my mom until the sub arrived. Wow, what dedication. Of course, this just added to my peace of mind.

The second set of what-ifs, which I did not think of initially but later clearly became an issue, had more to do with house maintenance. Late one night I got an e-mail telling me that the toilet the aides used was backed up, and they could not get it to work after using a plunger. Did my mother have a plumber? Well, she never had a problem with the plumbing before. So I called and e-mailed her neighbors to get recommendations. Of course, because all of her neighbors worked and were busy with kids and their own lives, they did not respond particularly quickly. Just think how much time I could have saved if I had had a list of local service companies.

Think of all the other what-ifs having to do with house or car maintenance. If your parent's car is being used for doc-tors' appointments or for running errands and it needs to be repaired, will staff know where to take it? If the lawn needs to be maintained or the driveway plowed in the event of a snowstorm, will staff know whom to call? I learned the hard way that a list of repairmen and their phone numbers needs to be posted or kept with other important information. If your parent does not have a list of such service providers, you can call her neighbors and get referrals.

Lists with phone numbers will save you time and headaches down the road

Make a list of all service providers such as a handyman, plumber, electrician, car mechanic, yard man, and snow removal service. (See sample sheet in Appendix B.) Also, if you buy certain items in specific stores, make these lists as well. For example, we bought organic fruits and vegetables and my mother's favorite desserts at a health food store and other items at a regular grocery store. I made a list of which items were to be purchased in which store. This way you can be sure that your parent is getting the foods she enjoys.

Let everyone know where the hide-a-key is

Although my mother's house was always unlocked because many people came and went all day and night, some staff members liked to lock the house at night during the 11:00 pm to 7:00 am shift. Therefore, some staff were concerned about locking themselves or someone else out. Because my mother was not ambulatory, this could have been a problem. So instead of giving everyone a key (something that I was not comfortable with), I bought a hide-a-key rock that fit in surprisingly well with the landscaping.

How to manage your parent's money for everyday expenses

The first step: you or one of your siblings must have a joint checking account with your parent. This is vital in case your parent has a stroke or some other event that would render them incompetent or unable to write checks.

It also should be decided among the siblings who will be responsible for managing the bills and other paperwork, such as putting together all of the documents for the tax preparer. If there is concern about potential abuse by the sibling or person designated to oversee your parent's finances, ask whoever is in charge to provide the rest of the family with monthly statements.

Once a parent is at home with multiple service providers, it is important to figure out how cash will be handled. Clearly you do not want to have a lot of cash sitting around. However, petty cash will be needed to buy supplies, food, prescriptions, and other items such as diapers, rubber gloves, body lotion, and toiletries. One way to reduce the amount of petty cash is through the purchase of gift cards, which can be used to buy food and pay for prescriptions and other health care-related items. Just ask that receipts be kept for each purchase.

Most stores have gift cards

I bought gift cards for the health food store and the drug store. Petty cash, which was kept in a separate envelope and was never more than $50, came in handy for paying the hairstylist when she came to the house or for buying items at other stores for which there were not gift cards. I also established an account with the owner of the home health care agency who monitored and replenished the petty cash fund.

We kept all the gift cards and petty cash in separate envelopes in a clear plastic storage box a bit bigger than a shoe box.

All of the meds, the pillbox, and all other important bits of information such as phone numbers were kept in this box to make it easier for the various staffers who handled the gift cards and meds. Clear plastic storage boxes can be purchased at Wal-Mart or Target, or office supply or home improvement stores.

Managing your parent's bills

All of my mother's mail was forwarded to me. Many months before my mother got sick, we established a joint checking account, knowing that the time would come that she would not be able to pay her bills.

Set up a joint checking account before your parent gets sick

Make sure you get checks printed with both your name and your parent's name on them. I neglected to do this and there was a delay in paying the bills, as I had to wait for the new checks to arrive. If you have siblings, make sure everyone is on board and that they are comfortable with the person designated to take care of your parent's financial affairs.

Of course, you can also set up online bill paying or use one of your parent's credit cards. Because my mother did not have any credit cards, I found it to be less cumbersome to just pay her bills the old-fashioned way, with checks.

Another option is to set up a separate checking account just for your parent's expenses. Depending on your own financial situation you might be able to afford to fund it, or you can ask that your parent fund it. Your parent generally knows what her monthly bills are, and she could fund this account for a few months at a time. Such a system can work while your parent is still lucid and somewhat well. However, once in-home care becomes part of the picture, the bills add up very quickly, and you may find that other arrangements will need to be made.

Decide what to do about the mail

If all the mail is forwarded to your address, then people cannot send get-well cards directly to your parent. The way I resolved this was by making arrangements with a neighbor for cards to be sent to my mother in care of them. *It takes two to three weeks after you have requested a change of address with your local post office before any mail is forwarded.* I did not know this; consequently, many bills were paid late the first month I took over paying my mother's bills.

What to do about valuables and financial papers

My mother's house, although quite modest in size, was often referred to as a museum, because she owned several large oil paintings from Europe, statues, lots of sterling silver trays, tea sets, and flatware. Before the first round of home health aides started to work for my mother, each time I visited I took some of her valuable jewelry home with me. What jewelry remained was very well hidden.

> ### Before you sign a contract, you MUST ask the home health care agency if their staff is bonded
>
> Before I talked with the owner of agency number 2, I was prepared to put all of my mother's valuables (that is, anything that was light enough to be hauled off) into the guest room and put a lock on the door. But after meeting with the owner, she assured me that they had been in homes like my mother's and that they were bonded and had no history of anything being stolen. All I needed to do was to avoid tempting workers by leaving small items such as rings, earrings, or cash lying around. This was great news, as it was one less thing I had to worry about.
>
> I also removed all of my mother's checkbooks, bank statements, and financial statements from her house. I doubt that the aides would have snooped around looking for such documents, but I had more peace of mind knowing that they did not have access to them.

Communicate, communicate, communicate

Regardless of where your parent is — at home, in rehab, or in a nursing home — it is essential that you stay in touch with the care providers. Even if you have the best possible care, letting the staff know that you are vitally interested in the daily care of your parent does help keep them on their toes. While my mother was in rehab, I spoke to at least one person a minimum of 5 days a week. Some days I checked in with the nurse or the charge nurse, and other days it was the social worker. If your parent is in a facility, it is helpful to talk with various staffers, as each offers a slightly different perspective.

After my mother came home and was in in-home hospice being taken care of by CNAs, I e-mailed or phoned the owner of the home health care agency on a regular basis. I also stayed in touch with my mother's hospice nurse, talked with the home health care aides, and of course was in contact with my mother. Because the elderly often view their situation through a different lens, sometimes getting input from a caregiver provides a more accurate picture of the actual situation.

It's vitally important that your parent's legal documents are in order

Before your parent becomes incapacitated or gravely ill, encourage her to ask her attorney to prepare all of the necessary legal documents and make sure that they have been properly signed and executed. If she decides that she wants a living will, it might be helpful to go over it with her to ensure that you fully understand her wishes. Also, ask her to show you where she has filed these documents as you never know when you will need them. And finally, it is always a good idea to have an extra copy for your own records.

An overview of various legal documents

Health care proxy a.k.a. health care power of attorney a.k.a. medical power of attorney

Your parent must appoint a health care power of attorney/ medical power of attorney/health care proxy

Depending on which state you live in, the term used to designate the person who has the authority to make medical decisions on behalf of another can be called a health care proxy, health care power of attorney, or medical power of attorney. As our parents age, we often have discussions about what they would like us to do for them in the event that they experience a catastrophic illness or accident or become incapacitated. More often than not, a parent appoints one of their children as health care power of attorney. Because it is a legal document, it is usually drawn up by an attorney. The role of the health care power of attorney is to communicate the wishes of the parent in the event that she is incapacitated and unable to make medical or health decisions. *However, in order for you to exercise your authority as health care power of attorney, you must have a copy of the document with you.* Some attorneys provide a business-size card that you can carry in your wallet. In my case, I carried a copy of this document with me whenever I visited my mother. *If you do not have a copy in hand, your voice will not be heard and your parent's wishes may not be carried out.*

I actually learned about this inadvertently while talking with a social worker from the Visiting Nurses Association (VNA) who had come to visit my mother while she was in palliative care. Had we not had this discussion, I would never have known about this policy and might have found myself in a very difficult situation, as I had no idea where my mother had placed her copy of the health care proxy.

If your parent has not appointed a health care power of attorney, encourage her to do so as soon as possible. We never expect the unexpected, so if she wants her wishes to be honored, she must have this document in place. Note: This document authorizes the designee to make only health-related and medical decisions in the event that the parent is declared incompetent or is incapacitated. The delegation of legal and financial decisions lies with the person holding a durable power of attorney.

Advance health care directives and living wills

Many people who are terminally ill or who have a life-threatening injury may choose to prepare an advance health care directive, which allows them to make their own decisions regarding the care they would prefer to receive. An advance health care directive is a legally binding set of instructions that explains the kind of medical care a person wants or does not want if she is no longer able to make those decisions. In many cases, an advance care directive limits the use of artificial support and may include a Do Not Resuscitate (DNR) order stating that the patient is not be revived if her breathing or heartbeat stop. Such a directive is particularly important if there could be disagreement among family members who may be having trouble letting their parent go. As a caregiver, following the final wishes of your parent is one of the most important things you can do to help her die with dignity and with peace of mind.

The importance of having an advance health care directive cannot be overstated. In 2002, the CDC's Healthy Aging

Team, in collaboration with the Association for Chronic Disease Directors (NACDD), developed 103 public health priorities for end-of-life issues. Among the top five was an initiative to educate the public about the importance of having advance health care directives and health care proxies.

Caring Connections provides free advance health care directives for each state. For more information, visit http://www.caringinfo.org/stateaddownload.

> If you find that you need to call 911, and if your parent has a DNR but it is not posted or is not available, emergency personnel in some states are legally responsible for administering cardiopulmonary resuscitation (CPR). Such life-saving measures may be contrary to your parent's wishes.

A living will is a written, legal document that conveys a person's wishes in the event of a terminal illness or a life-threatening injury. Like an advance health care directive, it may also provide instructions regarding the administration or withholding of lifesaving measures. It may include or exclude specific procedures, care, or treatment such as:

- CPR (if cardiac or respiratory arrest occurs)
- Supplemental nutrition through a feeding tube or IV
- Prolonged maintenance on a respirator (if unable to breathe unassisted)
- Invasive diagnostic tests such as spinal taps, blood gases, endoscopy
- Blood transfusions

Benefits of having an advance health care directive or living will:

- Promotes peace of mind
- Prevents costly specialized interventions that your parent does not want
- Reduces overall health care costs
- Allays feelings of helplessness and potential guilt among family members
- Puts to rest legal concerns for everyone involved

State laws vary regarding living wills; therefore, it is advisable to get information on how your state views living wills. This information can usually be obtained from your state's Bar Association, Medical Association, or Nursing Association, and most hospitals and medical centers.

Durable power of attorney

Your parent must appoint a durable power of attorney (POA)

If your parent appoints you or one of your siblings to serve as his or her durable POA, you or your sibling will be authorized to make *business and financial decisions* in accordance with your parent's wishes. However, please note: you *cannot* make decisions about your parent's health or health care. There must be a separate health care proxy document that authorizes an individual to make decisions about medical treatments and procedures. Depending on the circumstances, your parent may choose to have the same person serve as both the health care proxy agent and the durable POA agent. If your parent prefers, these roles can be filled by different people. Sometimes one sibling is more savvy about financial and business affairs while another may be better suited to deal with health care issues.

As with appointing a health care proxy, the sooner someone is appointed as a durable POA, the better. If your parent has all of their ducks in a row, everyone will have greater peace of mind.

Sometimes the discussion regarding the appointment of the health care proxy agent can segue into a discussion about a Do Not Resuscitate (DNR) order. A DNR is an order that states no effort will be made to use CPR if the person stops breathing or her heart stops beating. For example, if a person has a heart attack, electric paddles will not be used to stimulate the heart and establish a normal heart rhythm. A DNR can be issued by your parent's primary care physician. Your parent fills out the form, signs it, and sends it back to the primary care physician, who then signs and dates it and sends it back to your parent.

DNR

A DNR is supposed to be posted on the refrigerator door, as this is where paramedics are trained to look for it. Because my mother was quite active when she first got her DNR, I refused to post it on the refrigerator door. It seemed to me that it would be a constant reminder of her impending death. Most of us open the refrigerator door many times a day, and I could not imagine my mother having to look at this document day in and day out. We posted it in the den where it was visible but not in her face. Her home health aides and neighbors knew where it was. I suppose there could have been an instance in which having it in the den may not have served her well, but fortunately such a scenario never played out. However, once she became bedridden, we did post it on the refrigerator door.

> If your parent is admitted to rehab or to a nursing home, the facility must have the original DNR document. A photocopy will not do. Be sure to reclaim it when your parent is discharged.

Learn as much as you can about your parent's medical needs

Do you know what medications your parent is taking? Are you familiar with which ones cause side effects? Have you attended her medical appointments? Do you know if she is following medical protocols established by her physicians?

The first thing you need to do is to go over all medications with your parent and see if she is actually taking them and if they are still current. If she isn't taking them, ask her why. The consequences of noncompliance or nonadherence, that is, when people do not take their medications, are a major public health challenge. The reasons for noncompliance vary from simply forgetting to take one's medicine, to not wanting to experience side effects associated with a particular drug, to simply not being able to pay the astronomical costs of the prescription. According to the National Council on Patient Information, the economic burden of noncompliance costs the U.S. billions of dollars each year.

Because most clinical drug trials include patients between the ages of 18 and 65 years of age, very little is known about how the very elderly (adults in their 80s and 90s) actually metabolize drugs. And because their metabolism is slower than that of a younger person, if there is a side effect, it may last longer as the drug slowly works its way out of the system. Many physicians are not trained in gerontology and may not take into account the fact that greater caution is needed when prescribing drugs to this population.

Sadly, many doctors are not terribly interested in treating the elderly. Let's face it — their care tends to be more complicated than that of younger patients. They often suffer from multiple conditions such as high blood pressure, diabetes, high cholesterol, and congestive heart failure, and many elderly are a bit confused, so self-reporting is often inaccurate. Throw being hard of hearing into the mix, and the medical appointment becomes an exercise in futility. As accurate reporting is vitally important for the doctor to know what is actually going on, someone should accompany your parent to doctors' appointments. Don't be bashful about taking notes. Having a record of what was said will help if you or your parent have questions later on.

Drug interactions

Because seniors often have more than one condition for which they are taking medications, one of the most dangerous problems they face is drug-drug interaction. And because they often have more than one doctor who is prescribing drugs for them, unless each doctor has a list of all of their meds, they may prescribe a drug that will not fit into the mix.

Generic versus brand

To add to the potential for error, some physicians prescribe drugs using the brand name, while others use the generic name. For example, many elderly suffer from hypertension or congestive heart failure and may be prescribed Lasix, a common brand name. However, the generic name is furosemide. So if one physician prescribes Lasix and another furosemide, it is possible that your parent will think these are two different drugs. Adding to the confusion is the fact that the pills do not look alike.

Even younger adults who are functioning normally and are not suffering from any cognitive impairment could easily believe that these are two different drugs and inadvertently double the dose. In the case of Lasix, doubling the dose could lower one's blood pressure too much, and the person could feel faint after standing up too quickly or could feel weak in general, thus being at greater risk for falling. Doubling the dose of some other medications could result in even more serious consequences. (See Sample Prescription Log in Appendix B.)

Compliance

Studies show that older adults do not take their pills regularly, at least in part because they often have multiple prescriptions. Some medications are taken once a day, some two or three times a day, some with food, and some without food. If you find that your parent is having difficulty remembering which pills to take and when to take them, buy a med box with multiple timers and reminder alarms, or look into purchasing MedSignals, a new electronic pillbox described on page 62. Make sure your parent knows how to fill the med box. If she needs assistance, see if a neighbor or friend can help her out. Most med boxes need to be filled just once a week. MedSignals can hold a 1-month supply of up to four different medications.

Prescription bottles can also be color coded to reflect times of day. Colored dots can be bought at any stationary or office supply store and placed on the prescription bottle tops to serve as a reminder of which medications need to be taken when and which ones need to be taken with or without food.

Tell your parent or the person who is coordinating her medical care always to ask for a generic or to ask the doctor for samples.

What you need to know about pain management

If your parent takes pain meds, be sure their pain is well managed. There is still a concern that patients will become addicted to opioids, even when using them appropriately. This fear among health care providers can lead to under-prescribing.

According to Dr. James Campbell, a neurosurgeon at Johns Hopkins, opioids are more effective than any single class of drugs for chronic pain: "Opioids are fairly well tolerated, and unlike certain anti-inflammatory agents, they do not damage the liver or kidneys or lead to ulcers the way aspirin can." He believes that many doctors who are afraid to prescribe opioids are clinging to outdated conventions, such as the belief that they inevitably cause addiction or intolerable side effects.

"Opioids are among the most stigmatized medicines," says neurologist Dr. Russell Portenoy, chairman of pain medicine and palliative care at Beth Israel Medical Center in New York and president of the American Pain Society. "There is an enormous number of myths and misconceptions that physicians and the public perceive. Physicians need to know that if these medications are used properly, prescribing them is as routine as prescribing a blood pressure medicine. It doesn't need to carry any more of a stigma."[12]

The quality of one's life is contingent on proper pain management. Opioids should not be reserved just for end-of-life pain management, but should be seriously considered for elderly patients with persistent pain.

If your parent's pain is not well managed by taking over-the-counter anti-inflammatories such as Advil®, Tylenol, or aspirin, don't be afraid to talk with her doctor about prescribing opioids. If the doctor is reluctant to do so, then get a second opinion.

Remember that if opioids are prescribed, your parent may need to take some measures to avoid the constipation that often comes with opioid use. She might need to increase fiber and fluid intake or add a stool softener and a bulking agent like Metamucil® to her diet.

Coordination between the in-home health care agency and hospice — make sure the roles are delineated

As with any business or organization, you can have too many cooks in the kitchen. If your home health care organization is run by a nurse and there is also a hospice nurse, one of them must take on the role of case manager. In my mother's case, the hospice nurse was the hub of the medical team. She was responsible for filling the med box weekly, taking vital signs a couple of times a week, and reporting any changes in my mother's status to the primary care physician and to the director of the home health care agency. If there was a change in meds, she communicated this to the director of the home health care agency and noted the change(s) in the log book so that the aides were aware of them. She also was responsible for refilling prescriptions and for ordering medical supplies as they became needed.

If your parent is in in-home hospice, it might be better for the hospice nurse to be in charge of the medical care. Hospice nurses know what is covered by Medicare and can order hospital/medical equipment as the need arises. For example, as a patient becomes weaker, the hospice nurse might order a raised toilet seat with bars, a wheelchair, a portable commode, or oxygen.

If your parent is bedridden

If your parent is bedridden, proper skin care floats to the top of the list. To make sure that your parent maintains a good quality of life, skin breakdown must be avoided. Preventing bed sores supersedes all other concerns. The two main causes of bed sores are poor hygiene (that is, your parent is not changed in a timely manner) and lying in one position for more than two hours at a time. Patients need to be turned every two hours, 24 hours a day. This can sometimes be difficult during the night, but it must be done. The CNA should document in the patient log book that she turned your parent.

My mother was very stubborn about being repositioned. Fortunately for her, even at 95 years of age, her skin was able to withstand being in one position for weeks on end. To try to motivate her to be turned, I drew her a picture of a bed sore (as they say, a picture is worth a thousand words), but she simply was not comfortable on her side and was totally noncompliant. Lying on one's side is the better position in terms of preventing bed sores, as the areas most vulnerable are the tailbone, buttocks, elbows, and heels.

Bed sores are not only terribly painful, but can be life-threatening in the elderly

If you have ever talked with someone who has had to deal with a persistent bedsore, they will often tell you that it was the most agonizing aspect of their illness. Even people with cancer, who are in a lot of pain and take massive doses of pain killers, report that their pain meds simply did nothing to relieve the excruciating pain of their bed sore. So whatever the staff can do to prevent a bedsore from occurring in the first place, the better off your parent will be. The best prophylaxis is to make sure that the staff repositions your parent every two hours, that extra precautionary measures are taken for the most vulnerable areas such as the coccyx, buttocks, elbows, heels, and toes, and that your parent's skin is kept clean and dry. They should also make sure that there are not bulky folds in your parent's night clothes, and that the sheet is taut. Using laundry softeners can also help minimize the chance of getting bed sores.

When my mother came home to hospice the first time, we had a hospital bed that had an air mattress with a pump that kept the air moving all the time. Theoretically, by providing a mild constant massage, the air mattress increased her circulation and thereby reduced the possibility of getting bed sores.

Your role as parent care coordinator (PCC)

I have coined the term "parent care coordinator" (PCC) because this is a role that goes beyond that of an advocate and is more than that of a case manager. It is the umbrella that embraces all of the pieces of the health care delivery system, the glue that keeps the pieces intact, the voice that makes sure all of the parties involved are communicating. The PCC must be the parent's advocate as well as the case manager. He or she must be assertive as well as congenial and must know when to complain and when to sit tight.

As your parent's PCC, your primary goal is to find the best care available and to make sure that the agency you hire and the system you put in place can work smoothly on their own. The role of the PCC is enormously time-consuming and is enmeshed with many, many details. It requires planning and constant communication. If you are part of the Sandwich Generation and have a lot of other responsibilities, I suggest that you hire someone to fill this role, as coordinating all of the pieces of your parent's care plan can be a full-time job. Before you know it, you will find yourself deep in the belly of a beast that has an insatiable appetite for your time and can leave you feeling overwhelmed.

The responsibility of the PCC starts long before your parent needs assistance. It may begin with accompanying your parent to doctors' appointments, becoming familiar with all of her medications, learning about support services in the area, knowing which are the better rehab facilities in case your parent may require one, planting the seed that she may soon need assistance, and observing her closely, looking for any changes, even small ones, in her mental or physical status. Perhaps your parent is becoming more forgetful or is repeating herself. She may be having balance issues or experiencing shortness of breath while walking or going up a flight of stairs. Make note of these changes and discuss them. Does your parent tire more easily? Is she napping more? These are all signs that she may need someone to at least check on her, if not actually start helping her with simple chores such as cooking or even activities of daily living (ADLs).

As the PCC, it is your role to gently but firmly help your parent understand when it is time for her to have assistance. Having done your homework first and being able to present all the options at once will help both of you to decide which model will be the best fit. Included in your discussion should be in-home care and Meals On Wheels, as well as the use of systems like QuietCare and other passive monitoring devices or technological aides. And of course your role as a PCC will evolve as your parent's needs change. I cannot stress enough the importance of this role if you want to help your parent age in place.

Once you get some assistance, even if it starts out as just six hours per week of CNA care plus one of the passive monitoring systems, I can assure you that it will give you peace of mind. Many of us do not have the time to call our elderly parent daily. Yet, if she lives alone, you always are wondering if she is okay. And what is even worse is if she doesn't answer the phone after you have been calling all day. Talk about going into panic mode! By having aides going in a few days a week or installing a passive monitoring system, you can take comfort in the fact that someone is checking in on her and that her daily activities are being monitored around the clock.

> If you are the person coordinating your parent's in-home care, then as part of your role as PCC, I encourage you to call or e-mail her care providers daily. If your parent is in rehab recovering from an event, then you must also stay on top of her medical care. You may feel like you are being an annoyance, but if the staff know you are going to be active in managing your parent's care, they may make more of an effort to deliver better services.

The importance of extra pairs of eyes and ears, particularly if you live far away

I have already described the role of the PCC, which includes advocacy. But who is looking out for your parent's best interests when you are back home? Unless you are in a position to visit your parent every couple of weeks or you can rely on your parent's friends and neighbors to do so, you will need to find a friend or someone from church, or even hire someone (possibly someone from the senior center), who can check in on your parent, particularly if she is in rehab.

While my mother was in rehab, she was afraid to complain, because she feared retaliation. When she first was admitted, she was very unhappy and complained a lot. I was told by one of her nurses that my mother was making it difficult for the staff and that perhaps I should find another facility. The thought of having to find another facility that met all the requirements, plus moving my mother, who was still in a lot of pain from her broken pelvis, seemed daunting. So I told my mother not to complain, as it was affecting the care she was receiving. But then when there really was something to complain about, she didn't. In part, I suppose this was my fault.

I had already spent an entire month in Massachusetts and was only going to be in town for a few more days. Had I known that my mother was going to fear retaliation, of course I would have made some other choices. In any event, if you cannot oversee your parent's care, you need to have someone who can speak on her behalf.

If your parent has a lot of friends who are visiting, then they can become your eyes and ears. If not, then be sure to find someone to speak up for her. Some rehab facilities have ombudsmen. If you cannot monitor the care your parent is receiving in rehab, you should ask the ombudsmen to help out.

If your parent is being cared for at home, it is good if you can get feedback from visitors who just drop in. They can give you the scoop, as sometimes the aides act a bit differently while you are visiting versus when they are there unsupervised.

Nobody can do it all: when to consider hiring a geriatric care manager

With the surge of baby boomers coming of age, coupled with the increased desire of seniors to remain in their homes, a relatively new profession has emerged: geriatric care management. Today many seniors live far from other family members, or if family members are nearby, they may already be overwhelmed with having to take care of their own families and earn a living. As much as we might want to be the person in charge, sometimes circumstances require that we hire someone to coordinate the complexities of our parent's care.

A geriatric care manager (GCM) is a professional with specialized knowledge and expertise in senior care issues. Ideally, a GCM holds an advanced degree in gerontology, social work, psychology, nursing, or a related health and human services field. They evaluate your situation, identify solutions, and work with you to design a plan for maximizing your parent's independence and well-being. GCMs facilitate the care selection process for family members who live at a distance from their elderly relatives, as well as for those who live nearby but do not know how to tap into the appropriate local services.

You can hire a GCM for a single, specific task, such as helping you find a daily caregiver, or to oversee the entire caregiving process. In addition to helping seniors and their families directly, a GCM can be a liaison with other professionals who are an integral part are part of your parent's care and life, such as attorneys, physicians, social workers, home care companies, and others.

Many of us take on the role of the GCM by default, because we are the one who knows our parent the best. We are aware of her physical and mental status, we know what medications she takes, we have accompanied her to doctors' appointments, we understand her emotional needs, and we know who to call when the driveway needs to be plowed or the garbage disposal is stuck.

In reality, no one can know as much as we do about our parent. Yet, because of a variety of circumstances, we may need to assign this role to someone else. If you find that there simply are not enough hours in the day, or that you are so stressed out that it is affecting your health or your family life, or if you live too far away, do yourself a favor and hire a geriatric care manager if you can afford one. Their fee is between $50 and $200 per hour, depending on which part of the country you live in.

The following provides a snapshot of what a geriatric care manager can provide:

- *Coordination of doctors' appointments and obtaining and filling prescriptions.* Many elderly have multiple health issues and consequently may see anywhere from five to eight physicians. It is not uncommon for an elderly parent to see a primary care physician, an ophthalmologist, a cardiologist, an orthopedist, an internist, and more. Doctors' appointments must be scheduled and coordinated, prescriptions must be obtained and filled, all of which is time-consuming.

- *Arranging in-home care and other ancillary services.* Because GCMs are familiar with available resources, the task of finding and arranging care is something they can do with great facility. For an elderly parent being cared for at home, in-home care has to be arranged. There is often a need for a visiting nurse, physical therapist, or occupational therapist; setting up these visits requires calling yet another agency. In addition, the family caregiver may need to find reliable medical equipment such as a walker, raised toilet seat, or a wheelchair. For low-income elderly, other support services may be available such as The Ride, Meals On Wheels, and the Housing Authority — three more agencies and three more phone calls.

- *Maintaining good relationships.* Once again, because GCMs are part of the broader network of health care services, they usually have already established many relationships with others in the field. So when something goes wrong, a solution can be put into place without delay or disruption.

- *Advocacy.* No one will ever know your parent as well as you, nor will they be as passionate as you are. When you go with your parent to medical appointments, you can often find yourself in the role of an advocate. You may raise questions that your parent would not even think of. You may question the wisdom of prescribing certain medications or tests. You may even ask for a second opinion. No one can fill your shoes. But if you cannot take on this role, then the next best thing you can do is to hire a GCM who can accompany your parent to doctors' appointments.

As our parents age, they often are not the best patients. Their memories may not be so sharp, they no longer are good historians, and often their hearing is impaired. So it becomes terribly important that someone attend medical appointments with them.

> **If you have the means but do not have the time to be your parent's PCC, then you may want to hire a geriatric care manager**
>
> Geriatric care management is a relatively new profession. Geriatric care managers (GCMs) basically act as social workers, with the added benefit that they can analyze financial, legal, or medical information and interpret it for family members so that they understand the options. They closely monitor your parent's condition and keep you in the loop. You can determine the frequency of how often you want to be updated. To find a GCM, go to the Web site of National Association of Professional Geriatric Care Managers at: http://www.caremanager.org.

Talking about death is not taboo

In the United States, prior to the 19th century, death was always public. Friends and family, and even passersby would enter the bedroom while the dying person said final good-byes. After the person passed on, he or she would be laid out in the living room and family and friends would visit. But with the emergence of modern hospitals, caring for the sick and dying at home soon became relegated to hospitals. We became germ-phobic and turned over the care of those in their final days and hours to the health care system. Once a family affair, death is now almost invisible. As a result, we have allowed ourselves to be removed from participating in and witnessing this transition — one that we all will make some day. And as with many things in life, we fear what we do not understand. We fear what is unfamiliar.

Because our society is so uncomfortable talking about death, we do not have a clue as to what the dying process is really like. Most of us have seen people die on TV or in the movies but have not witnessed the actual death of a person. And rarely does Hollywood depict what death is really like. Even when independent filmmakers try to introduce the realities, such as in a film produced several years ago by the BBC, it is either aired at a time when viewing is low or is simply banned. In an effort to shield us from the graphic details, Hollywood prefers to sugarcoat death or, at the other extreme, even glamorize it. And until we as a society are able to embrace the dying process, including the unpleasantries that can accompany death, the media will continue to paint an unrealistic picture so as not to offend our sensibilities.

Here are some of the changes that can occur during the dying process. The more you know, the better prepared you will be. Several days before my 90-year-old stepfather died, the expression on his face changed dramatically, so much so that it scared my mother. His skin had tightened, masking his wrinkles, and his ears and nose had become softer, thus appearing to have changed shape. The hospice nurse had referred to these changes as the "death mask." After a person dies, the eyes may be open (as seen in the movies), but also the mouth opens as the muscles used to keep it closed become lax. This is rarely seen on TV or in the movies.

A good friend of mine had been keeping vigil by his mother's bedside and left to get a meal. When he returned, she had passed away. The hospital staff had not yet noticed. When he saw her, he was disturbed to find that her mouth and eyes were open. However, learning later that it is normal for the mouth to be open gave him some comfort.

Coming to terms with your fears — and helping your parent come to terms with hers

Although some older seniors who are in their 80s and 90s have come to terms with end-of-life issues and have made their peace with dying, others will pull out all the stops to stay alive. And often their children, too, are champions of the no-holds-barred approach. Doctors often order procedures without discussing the costs or the risks and benefits.

According to the *Dartmouth Health Atlas,* New York University Medical Center in Manhattan spends $105,000 on a typical elderly patient with multiple chronic conditions during the last two years of life. In contrast, at the Mayo Clinic's main teaching hospital in Rochester, Minnesota, the cost is $53,432. Remember, these costs are picked up by Medicare. There is no way that these kinds of expenditures will be sustainable as baby boomers become eligible for Medicare.

The medical establishment lives by the mantra, "Everything that can be done will be done." This mantra is no longer serving the elderly population at large. Instead, heart-to-heart discussions about procedures, outcomes, and fears about death and dying are needed. The elderly need to know what their chances are of survival and their subsequent quality of life. For example, the reality is that less than 2% of people in their 80s and 90s who have CPR at home live for one month.[13]

In a move to do what is best for the elderly, the term "slow medicine" was coined by Dr. Dennis McCullough, a Dartmouth geriatrician. He advocates that the elderly weigh the facts and not make rash decisions, and that they discuss proposed treatment or procedures with their spouse and/ or children. After all, no one wants a protracted decline and prolonged dependence — what some call "death by intensive care." If certain procedures or treatments will not improve the quality of life and may in fact be the catalysts that initiates a decline, then perhaps it is better to look at quality over quantity.

In my mother's case, when her gastroenterologist wanted her to undergo another endoscopy, I was able to query him about the risks versus benefits. I was aware of the risks, perforation of her esophagus being the greatest, and had doubts about the benefits. In the end, it became apparent that performing the endoscopy would benefit the doctor's research. Well, thanks, but no thanks. By evaluating the pros and cons of proposed new medications or procedures, I was essentially practicing slow medicine. Slow medicine is a new concept and is not embraced by many doctors, at least not yet. Everyone seems to be in a rush these days.

My mother and I had many conversations about death and dying. She often asked me if I believed in life after death. These conversations inevitably led to fairly lengthy discussions that often included perspectives other than those of her church. She had outlived her five siblings, had buried two husbands, and of course many of her friends had already passed away. Raised as a devout Catholic, she went to mass daily while growing up in her native Poland. Her life, like all our lives, had its ups and downs, and there were certain things that she had done that she was not proud of. She was convinced that she would be punished for her sins. No matter how many times I told her that God is loving and forgiving, the catechism that had been etched into her soul for 95 years prevailed. I have often wondered if it was her fear of dying that brought her back from the brink of death after she broke her pelvis. I felt so badly for her as she was consumed with worry and anxiety. She was plagued by her fears, and there was nothing I could say or do to help her.

However, as she got closer to the end of her life, she seemed to have come to terms with the inevitable and was a bit more at peace. She received the last rites three times: the first time while in the hospital when she was under the influence of heavy-duty pain meds, the second time when she was lucid while in rehab, and the third time while at home in the care of in-home hospice. She finally felt that her soul had been cleansed, and for the first time I saw a calm come over her. When she slept she no longer looked fearful, worried, or angry. Her expression was one of serenity.

My friends who have elderly parents have asked me, "How can I bring up the topic of death and dying?" One way to ease into such a discussion is to talk about the non-emotional aspects such as estate planning. Is there an up-to-date will or a living trust, is there a living will, has someone been appointed power of attorney or health care power of attorney? It is important to know if they want to die at home, and if so, how do they envision themselves being cared for? Do they have the finances for in-home care? Do they own their home so they can take advantage of a reverse mortgage?

If your parent has a terminal illness or is in hospice, you may need to bring up the topic of a DNR, which can segue to talking about final arrangements. Does your parent want to be buried or cremated? If she does not have a burial plot, where would she like to be buried? Does she want to be an organ donor? Does she want to participate in the writing of her obituary?

If talking about death or final arrangements makes your parent uncomfortable, don't push it. Let it go and wait to see if there is another time when she may feel more at ease. Perhaps having her pastor bring up these delicate matters would be easier for her. Another approach is watching a movie together about the passing of someone. Movies such as *Steel Magnolias*, *Beaches*, *Love Story*, and *On Golden Pond* address this subject with sensitivity. If you have siblings or other family members, you should talk among yourselves about what might be the best way to bring up the topic again and who should take on this task. It is possible that your parent will never want to talk about anything to do with her death.

There is a saying that "people die as they have lived". This is generally true, yet it is also possible for people to change. Sometimes, later in life, particularly if someone has lived a rather rigid life or was quite controlling, there is an "aha" moment that frees them from this way of being.

My mother was quite controlling in life, and she wanted her death to be predictable. She would have much preferred to have had a preselected date, and she probably would have preferred choosing it. But that was not the hand she was dealt. However, she had a say in expediting her death by choosing to discontinue her blood transfusions. Without transfusions, she knew her anemia would eventually ravage her body.

Because each of us dies when it is our time, and because my mother's hematologist/oncologist could not offer her a timetable, without transfusions her decline could have taken anywhere from two months to a year. So even though she took a little control over her death, the best we could do was to keep her comfortable. She often asked why it was taking so long. She had come to terms with dying and for the most part had overcome her fear. Patience was never her strong suit.

Friends of mine who visited talked about dying with my mother, and the aides she trusted also had heart-to-heart conversations with her. I believe that being able to voice her concerns about dying and share her fears with various people helped her find an inner peace.

How wonderful it would be if everyone who is either terminally ill or already at death's door could die peacefully without fear, without worrying about being judged and without being terrified of what awaits them on the other side. Just imagine the stress that we impose upon ourselves when we go into that place of fear. How can people possibly die peacefully if in their hearts and souls they believe that they will be punished for their sins? Who among us has not sinned? No wonder the fear of dying is so pervasive.

One of the greatest gifts you can give your parent is to talk to her about death and allay her fears. If it takes receiving the last rites three times, as it did for my mother, to get her into a place of acceptance, surrender, and self-forgiveness, then by all means let her receive the last rites as many times as she needs to. Help her receive whatever it is she needs in keeping with her religious beliefs. This may be the last act of kindness that you will be able to do for your parent. And when all is said and done, when it is time for her to make the transition into spirit, crossing over to the other side will be easier if she has made the shift from being in a place of fear to being in a place of peace. Without fear constantly tugging at her soul, it will be able to embark upon the final journey with greater ease.

Some facts you should know

"Although 90% of people say they want to die at home (according to two Gallup polls), nearly 80% of people die in hospitals, nursing homes, and other institutions. Unfortunately the vast majority of elders who are facing their last days are not in a comfortable, soothing environment surrounded by loved ones; most are hooked to tubes and encircled by machines, glaring lights, and strangers. Research on how people die is scarce, but the studies that have been done, as well as firsthand accounts, make it clear that the majority of people today die in pain, struggling with a litany of symptoms." (*Talking About Death Won't Kill You*, Virginia Moore, 2001.)

If your parent wants to die at home, do what you can to make it happen. Being in a hospital, or even worse, being in an Intensive care Unit (ICU), is one of the harshest environments in which to die. The bright lights and constant loud noises in an ICU, coupled with strangers coming and going, being surrounded by new faces each day instead of the faces of loved ones, create an environment in which she simply cannot die peacefully. Contrast this with being in her own bed in a quiet, dimly lit, familiar room and being attended to by warm, caring individuals. Family and friends come to visit, hold her hand, give her massages, and honor her final wishes. Dying at home is about as good as it gets.

Did I inadvertently prolong my mother's life?

As the soul starts to withdraw and the body starts to shut down, the need for food diminishes. This is natural. So instead of encouraging your parent to eat, perhaps it is kinder to acknowledge that 1) she isn't hungry, and 2) she is ready to let go and prepare for her journey to the other side.

If you have ever lost a dog or cat, you know that this is precisely what animals do. They becomes less and less interested in food and eventually become so weak that they cannot even hold up their heads. Once you have acknowledged the tell-tale signs of the dying process, in your heart you know it is time to say good-bye and call the vet. This gradual decline is simply part of nature. Humans experience a similar decline.

While in rehab, my mother was given Megace®, an appetite stimulant. The hope was that she would eat better and therefore have more energy and strength for physical and occupational therapy. Megace worked like a charm, and her appetite improved immensely. It was amazing how much food she could chow down. However, after she came home and no longer received PT and OT, she was still on Megace. I had several conversations with the hospice nurse about keeping her on an appetite stimulant, given that she was on a downward turn and was in a hurry for her life to be over. However, one of the few things she still was able to enjoy was food, so we decided that, because she was deriving some pleasure from eating (in particular, her favorite desserts) giving her Megace was part of the plan to keep her comfortable.

In retrospect, if I were faced with making this decision again, I am not sure that I would have continued giving her Megace for as long as we did. She clearly wanted to die sooner rather than later, and in all honesty, I think the Megace may have prolonged her life.

The dilemma of appetite stimulants at the end of life

If your parent is on an appetite stimulant, check with hospice on a regular basis to determine if it is in your parent's best interest to continue taking it.

If she wants to expedite the dying process and if she has become uninterested in food, it may be kinder to withdraw the appetite stimulant from the drug regimen.

Neither I nor her aides encouraged my mother to eat more than she wanted. We let her call the shots. As she became weaker, she simply wanted liquids, in spite of the Megace.

Preparing for the inevitable

Because the passing of a parent can be rife with emotions, it is better to address certain tasks ahead of time, such as selecting a plot, making funeral arrangements, and writing a eulogy and obituary. Making a list of friends and family members (including their phone numbers and e-mail addresses) who will need to be called, as well as having names and numbers for a clergy member and the funeral home available, will alleviate some of the stress. If your parent is at home, the hospice nurse will be very helpful in terms of notifying the funeral home and telling them how long you would like your parent to remain at home before being taken away. If there are cultural practices to be observed, just notify hospice ahead of time so that they can accommodate your wishes.

Bearing witness — the interlude between here and the beyond

A few months after my mother died, the mother of a friend passed away while in a residential hospice. My friend commented on her experience being with her mother during her last days and especially during her final day, when her mother was in a deep sleep. The day her mother died, all my friend could do was hold her mother's hand, stroke her brow, watch her breathe, and talk to her.

Having been at the side of two parents during their final days and hours and watching them take their final breaths, I am only too familiar with this period. All you can do is just be there. Death is so unpredictable. Hospice provides a list of signs that are precursors to death, but just as in life, everyone is an individual so there is no one-size-fits-all formula. You often wonder if your parent knows you are there, as there may not be any visible signs of recognition on her part.

They say hearing is the last sense to go. My friend's mother was quite deaf for the last several years of her life, and so she wondered if this was going to be true for her mother as well. From my own experience and stories I have heard about other people's experiences, I actually think that hearing is still the last sense to go even if the person was deaf in life.

While my friend's mother was gravely ill and seemed to be hanging on by a thread, the hospice nurse asked her if there was anyone her mother was waiting for. The only person she could think of was her mother's sister, who lived in Florida and was also not well. So she called her mother's sister and put the phone to her mother's ear. Even though her mother was extremely deaf and in a deep sleep, her facial expression, which had been static for days, changed when she "heard" her sister's voice. My friend's mother died that afternoon.

My mother was also quite deaf and wore a hearing aid in one ear. She really needed one for the other ear as well, but she was too vain to wear two. However, when she was dying and was not wearing her hearing aid, I often spoke to her in almost a whisper, and oddly enough, she was able to respond appropriately. It was a rather strange experience.

As my mother's soul started its retreat and death was near, there was a serenity that took over the room and its occupants. During these last days, quite often there would be several people in the room stationed around my mother's bed. More often than not, they spoke in whispers so as not to disturb her or wake her up from her drug-induced stupor. Keeping the shades drawn and creating a quiet, peaceful atmosphere is a way to honor the dying and parallels the teachings in *The Tibetan Book of the Dead*. The more peaceful the environment, the easier it is for the soul to depart.

Making funeral arrangements ahead of time — when to write the eulogy and obituary

Once my mother decided to discontinue getting transfusions, we knew it was just a matter of time before she passed away. When it became evident that she was on a downward spiral, I decided it was time to write her eulogy and obituary. Being a perfectionist, I knew that I would probably be in a better position to try to capture her essence while she was still alive and while I was not caught up in the emotionality of her loss. I had no time constraints and could revisit these drafts from time to time at my leisure and tweak them when necessary.

By having taken care of details ahead of time you will be able to concentrate on the moment and be able to spend quality time with your parent. The following are some practical tips that may help you organize your time and focus your efforts on your loved one:

- Make a list of people your loved one would like to have visit in the final weeks.
- Although the moment of death cannot be planned, it is best to think about who should be present at or around the time of death. Decide whether a clergy member should be at the bedside.
- Make a list of phone numbers of people to call after death occurs and enlist the help of a friend or relative to make those calls.
- Choose a funeral home and notify them that a death is expected in the near future. If your parent is in hospice, the hospice nurse may call the funeral home for you.
- Notify hospital or hospice staff of cultural and/ or religious mourning customs. This may include such things as a list of who should be present before and after the time of death, and any special customs surrounding washing, dressing, or caring for the body after death.

> If your parent is nearing the end of life, making final arrangements and being organized before your parent dies can alleviate a lot of stress. Take the time now to write her obituary and eulogy, and make as many of the final arrangements as you feel comfortable making.
>
> This may include talking with the funeral home director, picking out a casket, ordering flowers, selecting music to be played during the viewing and the funeral, maybe selecting a plot — the list goes on. Attending to these tasks when you are not wracked with emotion will be easier than if you wait.

Ethics 101

What you need to know when the best-laid plans fail

My greatest wish for my mother was that she would die at home with dignity, free from pain and discomfort. After all, that is why she was in in-home hospice. But sometimes the best-laid plans can go terribly wrong. After watching my mother suffer for two days, I had a new appreciation for what it means to be truly merciful.

Although it is beyond the scope of this book to examine the ethics surrounding how best to maintain the comfort of someone who is dying and to determine what constitutes comfort, I feel it is important to look at the issues that challenge us to go outside our comfort zone.

The vast majority of us hope that we will have a good death, a death that is free from pain. As the body shuts down, the dying person can experience a host of symptoms including nausea, tachycardia (rapid heartbeat), shortness of breath, anxiety, confusion, chills, hallucinations, and yes, sadly, pain. With any luck, you and your loved one will have discussed how she wants to spend these last days and hours. For some, the kindest thing you can do is increase sedating medications, so that she can be comfortable and die in peace.

But this decision is not an easy one. Many physicians and nurses find themselves in a dilemma as they decide how best to treat patients facing end-of-life discomfort. Add to this any potential conflict among siblings and other family members, and the result might be to err on the side of caution, that is, what makes the caregiver and family member feel comfortable. But what about the person who is dying? What about her comfort?

This quandary for caregivers is due to the fact that sedating medications have a dual effect — they ease or end the symptoms associated with dying and also can cause vital signs to deteriorate. In essence, they hasten death. Thus, it is a moral dilemma: have they crossed the line? Did they euthanize the patient? But even if they may have inadvertently hastened death, is that the primary concern? Or does the focus really need to be whether they did everything in their power to offer comfort to the dying and if they allowed that person to die with dignity?

When I looked up the definition of euthanasia, I was surprised to learn what it means. Euthanasia literally means good death or easy death (from the Greek, "eu" meaning good and "thanatos" meaning death). The definition of a good death may vary from culture to culture and from religion to religion, but in the end the majority of us would agree that this is what we want for our loved ones and for ourselves.

When it comes to our pets, most of us are comfortable with the concept of euthanasia. After all, none of us want to see them suffer. Yet when it comes to humans, society takes a very different view in spite of the fact that according to Gallup in 2004, 69% of Americans said they approve the legalization of euthanasia.[14] When Elisabeth Kübler-Ross was asked about pending legislation governing euthanasia, she responded, "I find it sad that we have to have laws about matters like this. I think we should use our human judgment, and come to grips with our own fear of death. Then we could respect patients' needs and listen to them, and would not have a problem such as this."[15]

And even though the U.S. Supreme Court declared in 1997 that effective palliative care is the right of every citizen[16], **regardless of whether that care hastens death,** we still may hesitate. Perhaps it is because we live in such a litigious society. After all, even if we did everything by the book, there is always room for interpretation. Legal battles are long and costly both in terms of money and emotions, so most like to play it safe at the expense of the dying.

Because my mother's last couple of days were so difficult, I feel compelled to tell her story so that others might be spared what she experienced and the horror that my mother's aides and I witnessed. At the risk of sounding melodramatic, in all honesty I would not have allowed my dog to go through what my mother endured. Prior to this experience, I had not read anything about euthanasia regarding the termination of a human life, as it just did not seem like anything I would ever encounter. And because I was uneducated, I was totally unprepared.

So the question on the table is, how much sedation is the right amount and how much is too much? It is a question that even the experts cannot really answer. But when you are faced with such a decision, I strongly suggest that you listen to your heart and not your head.

My mother's story

My mother was nearing the end of her life and was in *extreme* discomfort before she died. She always had a flair for the dramatic, and much to my shock and dismay, she begged me to poison her. It was clear that she was in distress, so I immediately got on the Internet and looked up the Hemlock Society to see what I could find. However, their Web site just recommends various books such as *"Final Exit"* and *"The Good Euthanasia Guide"*, both by Derek Humphry. I felt so helpless knowing that time was of the essence, as her suffering was unbearable to witness. And the weekend was almost upon us, possibly making it even more difficult to buy the necessary "ingredients." I could not find anything on the Web about how to make various lethal concoctions. And had I found the appropriate recipes, would I have been able to acquire the ingredients in time? Even though there may have been legal consequences to this action, that possibility never crossed my mind. Ending my mother's suffering was my only goal.

As you know, hospice is primarily about providing comfort, particularly at the end of life. However, everything does not always go as planned, and not everyone responds to medications the same way. Because my mother had experienced side effects in the past to almost everything in the comfort pack, from the beginning I had asked hospice if they could provide me with alternative drugs. I was told that there were no alternatives but if they gave her Compazine® along with morphine, she would be okay. As it turned out, the hospice nurse incorrectly believed that if the morphine was given sublingually (under the tongue) it would not reach my mother's stomach, and therefore she would not suffer from nausea and vomiting. Unfortunately, the hospice nurse did not understand that opioid-induced nausea and vomiting is a result of triggering a certain part of the brain and has nothing to do with the stomach. Regardless of the route of administration, morphine will always cross the blood/brain barrier. Had my mother been given the Compazine® prior to the morphine, she may have been spared from being horribly ill.

The meds in the hospice comfort pack include morphine, which has analgesic and sedating effects and can be used to make the transition easier by alleviating some of the anxiety and pain associated with the dying process. You and your family members, in conjunction with the hospice nurse, can decide how much morphine should be administered. Making the dying person comfortable is the primary goal. The question of how much is enough and how much is too much is really not relevant. Easing suffering is the priority. Eventually my mother fell into a deep sleep and no longer was suffering. She rested comfortably for about a day and a half before she finally passed away.

Because my worst fears were realized, in part, because of my not being better informed, I simply want you to be better educated than I was. If plan A fails, is there a plan B?

CHAPTER 5

Guidelines and Questions To Ask Home Health Care Agencies, Rehab Facilities, and Hospice

How to select a home health care agency

Making plans for your parent's care should be done before she is in need of assistance. Preparing a health care plan for her is like drawing up a will. You know it needs to be done, and the sooner you tend to it, the better. Otherwise it sort of lingers in the back of your mind. Creating a health care plan in advance is quite similar, as it can be revisited and modified as circumstances change.

As I have said before, if you have the luxury of time, do your homework before you hire an agency. Ask your neighbors and friends if they know someone who works in the home health care system or if they know anyone who has hired an agency. This is always a good place to start. And don't forget: Get as many references as you can.

Before you sign on the dotted line, make the following inquiries and ask the following questions:

- Is the agency certified by Medicaid or Medicare?
- What state licenses does the agency have?
- Are they insured?
- How many years has the agency been serving the community?
- What are the levels of care provided? (Some agencies provide CNAs, nurses, and companions. If you need more than CNA care, be sure you find an agency that can meet your needs.)
- Is there a written treatment plan? Who gets a copy?
- How are agency employees hired and trained?
- Does the agency perform communicable disease screens for their employees?
- How is the staff compensated? Are they contract workers? Do they work less than 40 hours a week? Do they work 40 hours and receive benefits? Can they work overtime, and if they do, do they receive time-and-a-half?
- What is the smallest block of time for which the agency provides services?
- What are the tasks that the CNA can and cannot do? (You need to be perfectly clear about this so that your expectations will be met and you can make other arrangements in case they cannot perform a specific function. For example, in my

mother's case, they would not give her supposi-tories. When I asked how this would be handled when a family member was not at home to assist with this task, I was told the patient would simply go without. Good agencies are a bit more creative and can come up with ways to get around these kinds of situations.)

- What is the level of training of the CNAs?
- What kinds of background checks have been performed? Does the agency perform criminal background checks?
- Is the staff bonded?
- How do they handle petty cash?
- Will there be some kind of consistency? Will the same people be assigned? How many people will be part of the CNA team?
- If there is a personality conflict, or if there is a problem with a CNA, will he or she be replaced?
- Ask the agency if you can request certain indi-viduals and if they honor such requests.
- Will there be a schedule of who is assigned for each shift at least one week out?
- Will that schedule be given to my parent and a copy sent to me?
- Do CNAs receive orientation prior to starting their shift?
- What are the fees? (Call several agencies to get a sense of costs. In Massachusetts, the hourly cost for a CNA ranges from $16.50 per hour for a 3-hour block of time, to $18.50 per hour for a

1-hour block, to $25 per hour. Most agencies charge time-and-a-half for holidays. You may want to get a list of which days they consider to be holidays. The cost of skilled nursing care is between $60 and $85 per hour.)

- Do they guarantee that all shifts will be covered or will you need to find alternative care when they cannot meet the need?
- If a CNA gets sick or has a family emergency, how will that shift be covered?
- Is there a nurse on call to answer questions as they arise?
- Is the nurse available 24/7?
- Is there a case manager? If so, who is it? What are his or her credentials?
- Who reviews medications, and who interfaces with the physician?
- Who fills the med box?
- Who is in charge of prescription refills?
- How is information transferred from one care-giver to the next when shifts change?
- How often is the case reviewed by the team? Who is on the team?
- If the VNA is involved, how will the care be coordinated?
- If hospice is involved, how will the care be coor-dinated?
- Ask to see a contract before you hire anyone. Each agency has its own termination clause. Some agencies require a 24-hour termination notice while others require two weeks. In the

case of the more lengthy termination notices, find out the exceptions, such as death or hospitalization. If your parent is receiving 24/7 care, this termination clause could cost you close to $7,000!

- If the agency has a Patient's Bill of Rights, ask to see a copy.
- Does the agency handle third-party payments (insurance, Medicare, Medicaid)?
- And, most importantly, ask for references. Make sure you call several people to find out if they were happy with the care they received from this agency.

If you are receiving 24/7 CNA coverage, the reality is that many different CNAs will be traipsing through your house. Some will be a better match for your parent than others. It is highly likely that you or your parent will not be happy with all of them. All you can do is hope that those who fit in best with your parent's needs and lifestyle will be assigned more often.

Note: Go to http://agingathome.info for free downloadable copies of various questionnaires.

Once you hire an agency, be sure to set some ground rules from the very beginning. Be clear about your expectations. If you have hired a private home health care provider, make sure that everyone is on the same page in terms of wages, hours to be worked, which days you consider to be holidays, etc. Go over the job responsibilities in detail. All of this should be in a contract that you and the caregiver both sign.

If your parent follows a routine, be sure to let the caregiver know. Your parent may prefer to have breakfast before she showers or to bathe before she goes to bed — whatever her preferences are, make sure they are known. Routine can be comforting for the elderly.

Certain rooms in the house, such as other bedrooms, a den, family room, or an office, might be off-limits. Let the caregivers know how much of the house they will have access to.

There may be other schedules that the caregivers will need to be aware of, such as the time of day that Meals On Wheels are delivered, so the food will be put into the refrigerator promptly. If the aides are responsible for putting out the trash, make sure they know what the schedule is and know which items get recycled.

If you or your parent are displeased with a particular CNA, let the agency know and ask that they send someone else.

How to select and deal with a rehab facility

If there is an ombudsman or patient advocate in your area, give them a call and see if he or she can recommend a facility. Sometimes the ombudsman will give you the names of the top two or three out of several facilities. In some cases, different states provide a ranking of which facilities meet various state and federal standards. Make sure to find out if any of these facilities have changed hands since the reports were written, as quite often a new owner will make drastic changes and improvements. The reverse can also be true. The rehab facility my mother was in was ranked at the bottom of the heap of about 500 facilities in Massachusetts in 2004, yet was considered to be one of the best in the area when she was a patient in 2006. So, once again, do your homework.

The discharge social worker at your local hospital is another valuable resource for finding out which rehab facilities have a good reputation. If you find that your parent needs to go to rehab directly from the hospital, the social worker can recommend some of the local facilities. I am not sure what they base their recommendations on, as the facility my mother ended up going to was not on their preferred list. However, I found that it met some of the criteria I was looking for while many of the facilities on their list fell short.

Rehab services can be found in either stand-alone facilities or as part of the services offered by nursing homes. When they are in a nursing home, one floor is usually dedicated as the rehab floor.

More than 1.5 million people live in nursing homes at a cost of more than $75 billion a year! With the new ratings system, the best nursing homes, like the best hotels, will get five stars. You can find a listing of the government's 5-star rating system at http://www.Medicare.gov/NHCompare. A Web site available at http://www.memberofthefamily.net provides user-friendly reports based on government inspections of the nation's 16,000 nursing homes. The site includes past and present survey results. The most useful tool on the site is the National Watch List, which lists nursing homes cited for violations or those that have received a substantial number of complaints. Memberofthefamily.net also provides an honor roll of facilities found to be deficiency-free.

Before you decide on a rehab facility, call and make an appointment

Ask to meet with the person in charge of admissions and either the social worker or the director of nursing. Don't forget — it is the job of the director of admissions to keep the beds full. They may not be as forthcoming or candid as the social worker or director of nursing. Tours given by the social worker or director of nursing can sometimes be more revealing.

When meeting with the director of admissions, ask if there are any vacancies. If so, how many? If not, how long is the waiting list? What is the maximum number of patients the facility can treat? How many CNAs and nurses are on each shift?

Ask about staffing ratios. Because federal guidelines recommend only RN and LPN ratios and do not address CNA/patient ratios, you will need to check with your state. Many states have guidelines that exceed federal RN and LPN levels, and more than half recommend CNA/patient ratios. Massachusetts recommends that patients receive 2.9 hours of CNA care each day (this is probably over a 24-hour period). Most facilities do not even come close to meeting this requirement. The rehab facility should be able to provide you with your state's guidelines. When looking at staffing ratios, remember that CNAs also deliver meals, which takes time away from giving one-on-one care.

In Congress, Representative Henry Waxman and Senator Charles Grassley reported in 2002 that 90% of nursing homes were unable to provide adequate care because of staffing shortages. Given the rising senior population, the problems cited in this report are likely to be worse today than they were in 2002.

While you are talking with the director of admissions, ask about Medicare to find out if your parent is eligible for at least some coverage.

Medicare

When my mother was in rehab, there were restrictions in terms of when Medicare paid for rehab and when the costs were the responsibility of the patient. In 2006, if the patient went directly from the hospital into rehab after having spent at least three nights in the hospital, then Medicare paid for rehab up to 100 days, paying 100% for the first 20 days and everything but $99 per day from days 21-100. My mother's supplemental insurance covered what Medicare did not pay. If the patient went home after having been hospitalized for three or more nights, there was a 30-day period during which the patient would have to enter a rehab facility if Medicare was to cover their expenses. It is best to check with the hospital social worker, as there are other considerations regarding Medicare, and the terms and conditions are always subject to change. Also check with your parent's supplemental insurance provider for specifics on her coverage.

Bring a list of questions

It is too easy to forget what you want to ask when you are interviewing the various staff members and taking the tour. You are trying to garner a lot of information as you walk through the facility. Your observation skills should be at their sharpest while you make mental notes of each area. Look for overall cleanliness, smells, and orderliness of common rooms and patient rooms. What is the prevailing atmosphere — do patients seem cheerful or depressed? What is the attitude of the staff and their supervisors? Are the staff rushing around? Are there lots of bells ringing or lights flashing for assistance? Does there seem to be enough staff?

The director of nursing and the director of admissions are unlikely to admit that there are any staffing problems. I asked the director of admissions from one of the facilities about their staffing ratios, and the numbers she provided indicated that they were well staffed. Perhaps they met those ratios on a good day. But people call in sick all the time. The boyfriend of one of my mother's aides was a CNA and often had as many as 17 patients to care for during his morning shift, which also involved serving two meals. Another of my mother's aides had applied for a job at the same facility, and during the whole time she was there, a patient was lying on the floor and no one came to the patient's aid. And this was a facility that was highly recommended.

While on your tour, ask to see the menu. It is usually posted in a central location so patients know what they can expect for lunch and dinner. Does the menu look appealing, or are there listings like chicken nuggets, sloppy joes, and hot dogs and beans? Good nutrition is a vital component of one's health, so it is important that your parent is getting food that is well-prepared, fresh, tasty, and nutritious.

If possible, visit the facility during mealtime. This will serve a double purpose. First, it will give you a sense of how stressed out the staff is during mealtime while serving a lot of people in a short period of time as well as attending to those who need assistance. Second, you will have a birds-eye view of what is being served. See if there are any fresh fruits or vegetables. Canned vegetables are pretty easy to spot. Are there salads? And is there a choice, or is everyone (except those on special diets) served the same fare? If you can, taste the food yourself.

Visit the dining hall and see if the residents are enjoying themselves. Are staff members available to assist those who need help with feeding?

Most facilities have one or two ombudsmen assigned to them. But only one of the four facilities I visited had the phone number for the ombudsmen posted next to the elevators where visitors could easily see it. If the facility is transparent and has nothing to hide, they likely are willing to post a number for an ombudsman in a conspicuous location. An ombudsman can be a godsend when you have to manage care from afar.

Every nursing home is inspected by state and federal agencies. Each agency issues a report on any deficiencies it finds at the facility. These reports are collected by the federal government, and a summary and comparison of the findings can be accessed at http://www.medicare.gov/NHcompare. The National Citizen's Coalition for Nursing Home Reform, at http://www.nccnhr.org, offers a consumer guide to choosing a nursing home.

Even good nursing homes will be cited for some deficiencies. It is important to assess their relative seriousness. Was the incident a one-time event or is there a pattern? Did the incident jeopardize the well-being of a patient?

One of the things you can ask the ombudsman is if the facility has had a lot of complaints filed against it. The ombudsmen will be glad to answer your questions and help you interpret the findings in the report.

> An ombudsman can be a lifesaver. If your parent is experiencing any kind of problem such as neglect, abuse, or poor care, call the ombudsman. The nursing home or rehab facility should have the name and number of the ombudsman posted in a conspicuous location. If you do not see it, you can find an ombudsman in your area by contacting your local state ombudsman office or by visiting http://www.ltcombudsman.org/static_pages/ombudsmen.cfm.

Other factors to consider when selecting a facility:

- Ask if they are Medicare certified. Ask if there is a large vacancy rate and if so, why? If not, ask if there is availability or if there is a waiting list.
- Ask if they are a for-profit agency. Who is the owner?
- If they are nonprofit, what is their affiliation?
- Ask if they are part of a chain.
- Ask how many nurse's aides there are per resident. You may want them to break this ratio down per shift.
- How much time per day do nurse's aides spend one-on-one with a patient?
- Do they allow the hiring of private CNAs?
- Ask about transportation costs to and from medical appointments. Because transportation to and from doctor's visits is calculated by the mile and is usually provided by an ambulance company that uses wheelchair vans, you may want to choose a facility that is not too far from your parent's physicians. If there is a family member who can shuttle your loved one, then this is not so much of an issue. Also, if your parent might be in pain while being transported, you may want to choose a facility closer to her doctors.
- If the facility is out of the jurisdiction of your parent's primary care physician, inquire about the medical director at the facility. Ask as many questions as you can to determine if you want

this physician to be in charge of your parent's
care.

- What sorts of activities are offered? Are there
  activities during the day and evening?
- What are the opportunities for socializing?
- Is there a living room or a common area in
  which patients can play games?
- Can patients choose to eat in the dining room?
- Are there more food choices if they eat in the
  dining room? (This was the case in the facility
  where my mother stayed.)
- Check out the physical therapy (PT) room — is
  it inviting or is it tiny?
- Are the physical and occupational therapists
  (PTs and OTs) contract workers or are they on
  staff? How long have they been at this facility,
  and how experienced are they?
- What measures have been taken to deinstitu-
  tionalize the facility?
- Are there fish tanks, cats, pet therapy dogs, avi-
  aries, etc.?
- Can family dogs come to visit?
- Does the facility offer a laundry service, or does
  someone have to collect laundry each week?
- Are bed linens and towels cleaned daily? Ask
  what the laundry department does to prevent
  bed sores (types of detergents, softeners used,
  etc.).
- While observing the facility, notice if there are
  soiled linens piled up in the hallways or in resident's rooms.

- Are the showers clean?
- Is there a hairstylist on site?
- How is petty cash managed? Can you set up an account?
- Are the patient rooms made to look more like bedrooms? How are they furnished and decorated? Can you personalize the room?
- What do you need to supply? Is there a TV and a phone in patients' rooms, or do you need to provide these?
- And finally, try to imagine yourself being there for one to three months or longer.

Another thing to keep in mind when selecting a nursing home/rehab facility is the proximity to your parent's doctor, hospital, family, and friends.

Some tips on buying clothes for rehab, particularly if they are going to be laundered at the facility

Because washers and dryers in rehab facilities are extremely hot, you can expect that 100% cotton clothes will shrink. Also, depending on whether your parent is incontinent, you may want to choose pants that are a size larger, as they will be easier to put on. Depend® products are not too bulky, but some of the other diapers are. If you have time to investigate different rehab facilities, they will tell you how many changes of clothing you need to bring for your parent. At the facility where my mother stayed, she wore a different nightgown each night, so I had to buy her a few more nightgowns to keep her well supplied.

All clothing must be marked with indelible ink if you ever hope to see it again, and of course that is not a guarantee. I made several trips to the laundry room to look for my mother's clothes and more often than not came back empty-handed.

How to select hospice

What is hospice?

The word "hospice" has been a household word for several decades, thanks to Elisabeth Kübler-Ross. However, the origin of hospice might intrigue you. Having the same root as "hospitality", the word hospice dates back to medieval times, when it referred to a place of shelter and rest for travelers who had become ill or were weary after a long journey. The first application of hospice in modern times was in 1967, when Dame Cicely Saunders, a British physician, founded St. Christopher's Hospice in London.

The concept of hospice was first introduced to the United States in 1963, when Dr. Saunders gave a lecture to medical students, nurses, social workers, and chaplains at Yale University. She showed before and after photos of terminally ill cancer patients and documented the dramatic changes seen in patients who received a holistic approach to their care, which included offering services to family members as well. Her lecture ignited the hospice movement as we know it today and over the years has resulted in making the transition from life to death much easier for many thousands of patients and their loved ones.

Hospice not only provides comfort to those who are in the last stages of life, whether from cancer or other terminal disease, but also offers support to the patient's family.

Patients are eligible to receive hospice services if their physician has determined that they have six months or less to live. Once a patient enters hospice, he or she agrees to terminate lifesaving treatment. For example, cancer patients no longer receive chemotherapy, or those with advanced anemia no longer receive blood transfusions. However, some hospices are re-evaluating their requirements, both in terms of allowing patients to receive treatment and regarding the 6-month rule. This is particularly important in residential hospices. If a patient does not die "on schedule," what happens next? Do you discharge a dying person?

There are several models of hospice care: in-hospital, in-home, and residential. Some hospitals have hospice wards where patients receive the same care they would if they were in a residential hospice facility. Smaller community and regional hospitals may not be able to dedicate a part of a floor for hospice, and thus the role of hospice is reduced to being able to provide only support and comfort to the patient's family.

Most residential hospices usually have a limited number of beds. Residential facilities are not available in all towns and cities, and because of the limited number of patients they can treat, the vast majority of patients receive hospice in their homes. In-home hospice is paid for by Medicare. The number of times the hospice nurse visits is determined by the needs of the patient. Generally, if a patient is stable, the nurse may come only once a week. Depending on the services provided by your particular hospice, the patient may also be assigned an aide in addition to a nurse.

When my mother was in hospice the second time, she was assigned a CNA who came for an hour and a half each day, Monday through Friday. We also had hospice volunteers who came on the weekends and helped with shopping.

Here are some things you need to know about hospice

First of all, there may be more than one hospice that serves your area. This was something that never crossed my mind.

When my mother came home the first time and was placed in hospice, the hospital set up her care with the group affiliated with the hospital. As chronicled earlier in this book, this hospice provided minimal services.

During the many months that I supervised my mother's care, I had quite a few opportunities to talk with many caregivers who dealt with hospice every day, and I heard numerous stories that were truly heartbreaking. For our parents to die with dignity and comfort, hospice must be better funded. Unfortunately, funding for hospice has decreased over the years, which, needless to say, impacts the quality of care. Unless there is active fundraising, the care can fall short of what you might expect. If there is more than one hospice in your area, find out which one is actively fundraising — they may be in a position to provide better services.

In the early weeks of care, depending on your parent's condition, more than likely your parent will not need someone there all the time. However, because one of the greatest fears expressed by many patients is the fear of dying alone, as death approaches, it is best to have someone by your parent's side while she is awake, and even when she is asleep if you can manage it. Although family, friends, and private care providers deliver most of the care, hospice provides volunteers to run errands and a CNA to either fill in the gap or relieve the caregivers. However, remember that they are not able to offer assistance for extended periods of time. Hospice does have staff members who are available around the clock for phone consultations and will come out to the house any time day or night if there is a crisis. (The first hospice I worked with DID NOT provide this level of care — make sure you ask before you sign on.)

Watching a loved one die is a very emotional and spiritual process. It is different for each of us. Some individuals want to be alone, preferring that no one else be there to interfere with the passing of our parent. Perhaps we have a ritual that we would like to carry out or a particular wish we want to honor. Some believe that the room should be dimly lit and very quiet so that the soul can exit peacefully.

If you and your family members are uncomfortable with death and dying, you may be terrified at the prospect of being alone while your parent is actively dying. What will you do if your parent goes into respiratory arrest, has episodes of vomiting, has hallucinations, or one of a myriad of other end-of-life experiences? Will you and your family members respond appropriately? Will you know how much morphine to administer? Will you be comfortable inserting anti-nausea suppositories? If not, then you will need a registered nurse, as a CNA is not allowed to do this. Be honest about what you will be comfortable doing, so that if you need professional help such as a private-duty nurse, you can make the necessary arrangements. No one can predict when or how death will occur. Each end-of-life journey is unique.

> Depending on your comfort level, you should plan ahead. If you know that hospice will not be there for extended periods of time, make sure that you and your family members and friends are prepared for the unexpected. Educate yourself as much as you can and read about death and dying so that you will not be surprised, shocked, or immobilized by what you are witnessing. If hospice does their job properly, you and your loved one should be in good hands.

Questions to ask hospice

Here are some questions that you may want to ask when looking for hospice:

- Who accredits them? The Joint Commission on Accreditation of health care Organizations or the state Department of Health? Being accredited by one of these organizations means that they voluntarily sought accreditation and are committed to providing quality care.
- Are they licensed? If so, by whom?

- What is their admissions policy? Must patients be referred to them by a physician? Are there specific criteria? Are they willing to explain to you what their parameters are and how your parent may qualify? If it is residential hospice, do they offer other services such as short-term respite?

- Are they certified by Medicare? To be certified by Medicare, they must have met federal minimum requirements for patient care and management.

- What are the costs, and how do they handle payment and billing? Before services are provided, you usually sign a contract that outlines what is going to be provided. They will leave a copy of the contract with you and take a signed copy for their records. Ask if they can assist your parent in finding financial assistance if needed. Also ask if there are payment plans. (Note: Residential hospice is expensive. In 2006, the residential hospice in my mother's little town in Massachusetts was $250/day. If your parent is indigent, the cost will be covered by Medicare.)

- Does the hospice require that there be a designated family primary caregiver as a condition of admission? How much flexibility do they provide? Will they work with you around your schedule? What can they offer for a parent who lives alone and whose family members are far away?

- Who is in charge of your parent's care? How is the staff trained? Are the caregivers licensed and bonded?
- Who provides the plan of care? Who monitors the plan of care? Who fills the med box? If there is a home health agency also working as part of the team, who ultimately has the final say? Ask if you can see a sample plan of care.
- Who conducts the preliminary patient evaluation? Is it done by a nurse or social worker or by the head nurse from the health care agency if there is such an agency in place? What does it highlight? Does it address what your parent can do for herself? Who is involved in the evaluation — your parent's primary care physician, family members, others?
- If you have a grievance, what is the procedure? What is the chain of command?
- Ask them how long they have been in business, and ask for references. Of course, if they are the only game in town and you need hospice, then this point may be moot.
- Ask them about their timetable for initiating services. How much lead time do they need?

By asking all of these questions, in essence, you are interviewing them. Take note of their attitude. Do they seem compassionate and caring? Watch them interact with your parent and think about how this interaction would make you feel if you were in your parent's shoes.

If they provide residential hospice, tour the facility and ask the following:

- What is the staffing ratio?
- How long can a patient stay?
- Who is in charge of their care?
- What are the visiting hours and can pets come to visit?
- If it turns out that your parent lives beyond the 6-month time limit, will she be allowed to stay? If not, what is the procedure for her to return home or go back to assisted living or the nursing home?

Appendix A

Questionnaire for Screening Home Health Care Agencies
(Download form at http://www.agingathome.info)

	Yes	No	Other Responses
Is the agency certified by Medicaid and/or Medicare?			
What state licenses does the agency have?			
Is the agency insured?			
How many years has the agency been serving the community?			
What are the levels of care provided? (Some agencies provide CNAs, nurses, and companions.)			
Is there a written treatment plan? Who gets a copy?			
How are agency employees hired and trained?			
Does the agency perform communicable disease screens for its employees?			
How is the staff compensated? Are they contract workers? Do they work less than 40 hours a week? Do they receive benefits? Can they work overtime, and if they do, do they receive time-and-a-half?			
What is the smallest block of time for which the agency provides services?			

Questionnaire for Screening Home Health Care Agencies
(Download form at http://www.agingathome.info)

	Yes	No	Other Responses
What can CNAs do? What can they not do? (You need to be perfectly clear about this so your expectations will be met and you can make other arrangements in case they cannot perform a specific function.)			
What is the level of training of the CNAs?			
What kind of background checks have been performed? Does the agency perform criminal background checks?			
Is the staff bonded?			
How is petty cash handled?			
Will there be some kind of consistency? Will the same people be assigned to my parent's care? How many people will be part of the CNA team?			
If there is a personality conflict or if there is a problem with a CNA, will he or she be replaced?			
Will there be a schedule of who is assigned for each shift for at least one week out?			
Will that schedule be given to my parent and a copy sent to me?			
Do CNAs receive orientation prior to starting their shift?			

Questionnaire for Screening Home Health Care Agencies
(Download form at http://www.agingathome.info)

	Yes	No	Other Responses
What are the fees? (Call several agencies to get a sense of costs, which can vary considerably. Most agencies charge time-and-a-half for holidays. You may want to get a list of which days they consider to be holidays. The cost of skilled nursing care is between $60 and $85 per hour.)			
Does the agency guarantee that all shifts will be covered, or will I need to find alternative care when the agency cannot meet a need?			
If a CNA gets sick or has a family emergency, how will that shift be covered?			
Can I request certain individuals?			
Is there a nurse on call to answer questions as they arise?			
Is the nurse available 24/7?			
Is there a case manager? If so, who is it? What are his or her credentials?			
Who reviews medications, and who interfaces with the physician?			
Who fills the med box?			
Who is in charge of prescription refills?			
How is information transferred from one person to the next?			
How often is the case reviewed by the team? Who is on the team?			

Questionnaire for Screening Home Health Care Agencies
(Download form at http://www.agingathome.info)

	Yes	No	Other Responses
If the VNA is involved, how will the care be coordinated?			
If hospice is involved, how will the care be coordinated?			
What is the termination policy? (Note: Ask to see a contract before you hire anyone. Each agency has its own termination clause. Some agencies require a 24-hour termination notice whereas others may require two weeks. In the case of the more lengthy termination notices, find out the exceptions, such as death, rehab, or hospitalization.)			
Does the agency have a Patient's Bill of Rights? May I see a copy?			
Does the agency handle third-party payments (insurance, Medicare, Medicaid)?			
Can the agency provide references? (Make sure you call several people to find out if they were happy with the care they received.)			
Notes/summary of answers:			

Questionnaire for Screening Rehab Facilities
(Download form at http://www.agingathome.info)

Note: Most interviews will be conducted with the director of admissions

	Yes	No	Other responses
Are you Medicare- or Medicaid-certified?			
Do you have a large vacancy rate? If not, is there is a wait?			
Are you a for-profit facility? Who is the owner?			
Are you part of a chain?			
If they are nonprofit, ask, "What is your affiliation?"			
Staffing			
How many nurse's aides are there per resident? (You may want them to break down this ratio per shift.)			
How much time per day do nurse's aides spend one-on-one with a patient?			
Do you allow the hiring of private CNAs?			
Do you provide transportation to and from medical appointments? What is the charge? (Note: Because transportation to and from doctor's visits is calculated by the mile and is usually provided by an ambulance company that uses wheelchair vans, you may want to choose a facility that is not too far from your parent's physicians. If there is a family member who can shuttle your loved one, then this is not so much of an issue. Also, if your parent might be in pain while being transported, you may want to choose a facility closer to her doctors.)			

	Yes	No	Other responses
What can you tell me about your medical director? (Note: If the facility is out of the jurisdiction of your parent's primary care physician, inquire about the medical director at the facility. Ask as many questions as you can to determine if you want this physician to be in charge of your parent's care.)			
Are the PTs and OTs contract workers or are they on staff?			
On average, how long have they been at this facility and how experienced are they?			
How often will my parent be evaluated by the team?			
How often will my parent be seen by the medical director? (If you do not know the medical director, ask to make an appointment to meet him or her.)			
Social Activities			
What sorts of social activities do you provide? Are there activities offered during the day and evening?			
What are the opportunities for socializing?			
Is there a living room or a common area in which patients can play games?			
Food			
May I see sample menus for breakfast, lunch and dinner?			
Do you provide fresh fruits and vegetables?			

	Yes	No	Other responses
Can patients choose to eat in the dining room?			
Are there more food choices if patients eat in the dining room?			
Do you serve the same food for dinner one night and then for lunch the next day?			
Measures taken to deinstitutionalize the facility			
What measures have been taken to deinstitutionalize the facility?			
Can family dogs come to visit?			
Do you have any resident pets? (Some facilities have cats, birds, or fish.)			
Laundry			
Do you offer laundry service or does someone have to collect it each week?			
Are bed linens and towels cleaned daily? (Ask what the laundry department does to prevent bed sores re: types of detergents or softeners used.)			
Miscellaneous			
Is there a hairstylist on site?			
How is petty cash managed? Can you set up an account?			
Observations			
Are the patient rooms made to look more like bedrooms? How are they furnished and decorated?			
Can you personalize the room?			

	Yes	No	Other responses
What do you need to supply? Is there a TV and a phone in patient rooms or do you need to bring these?			
Are soiled linens piled up in the hallways or in resident's rooms?			
Are the showers clean?			
Do the residents look happy?			
Do the residents look clean and well-groomed?			
Are there unpleasant odors?			
What is the physical therapy room like? Is it inviting? Is it tiny?			
Are there several patients doing PT at the same time?			
What is the occupational therapy (OT) room like?			
How are patients being treated by the PTs and OTs, gently and with care, or are they a bit rough?			
Proximity to doctors, friends, and relatives			
What is the proximity to your parent's doctor(s), hospital, family, and friends? You will want as many people to visit as possible, they will be your eyes and ears.			
And finally, try to imagine yourself being in this place for one to three months or longer.			

	Yes	No	Other responses
Notes/summary of answers:			

Questionnaire for Screening Hospice
(Download form at http://www.agingathome.info)

	Yes	No	Other responses
Are you accredited? If yes, by whom? The Joint Commission on Accreditation of health care Organizations or the State Department of Health? (Note: Being accredited by one of these organizations means that they voluntarily sought accreditation and are committed to providing quality care.)			
Are you licensed? If yes, by whom?			
What is your admissions policy? Do patients need to be referred by a physician? Are there specific criteria? Can you explain the parameters and how my parent may qualify? (If it is residential hospice, do they offer other services such as short-term respite care?)			
Are you certified by Medicare and/or Medicaid?			
What is the timetable for initiating services? How much lead time is required?			
Who is in charge of my parent's care? How is the staff trained? Are the caregivers licensed and bonded?			
Who provides the plan of care? Who monitors the plan of care? Who fills the med box?			
If there is a home health agency also working as part of the team, who ultimately has the final say? Can I see a sample plan of care?			

Questionnaire for Screening Hospice

(Download form at http://www.agingathome.info)

	Yes	No	Other responses
Who conducts the preliminary evaluation? Is it done by a nurse or social worker, or by the head nurse from the health care agency if there is such an agency in place? What does it highlight? Does it address what my parent can do for himself/herself? Who is involved in the evaluation—my parent's primary care physician, family members, etc.?			
If I have a grievance, what is the procedure? What is the chain of command?			
How long has this hospice been in business? Can I get some references? (Of course, if they are the only game in town and you need hospice, then this may be moot.)			
Residential Hospice			
Do you offer other services such as short-term respite care?			
What are the costs, and how are payment and billing handled? (Note: Before services are provided, you usually sign a contract that outlines what is going to be provided. Make sure they leave a copy of the contract with you. Ask if they can assist your parent in finding financial assistance if needed. Also ask if there are payment plans.)			

Questionnaire for Screening Hospice

(Download form at http://www.agingathome.info)

	Yes	No	Other responses
Do you require that there be a designated family primary caregiver as a condition of admission? How much flexibility do you provide? Will you work with me around my schedule? What can you offer a parent who lives alone and has family members who are far away?			
What is the staffing ratio?			
How long can a patient stay?			
Who is in charge of my parent's care?			
What are the visiting hours? Can pets come to visit?			
If it turns out that my parent exceeds the 6-month limit, can he or she stay on? If not, what is the mechanism either to return home or go back to assisted living or the nursing home? (Note: When you are asking all of these questions, you in essence are interviewing those who will be responsible for your parent's care. Do they seem compassionate and caring? Watch them interact with your parent. If you were in your parent's shoes, how would that interaction make you feel?)			

Appendix B

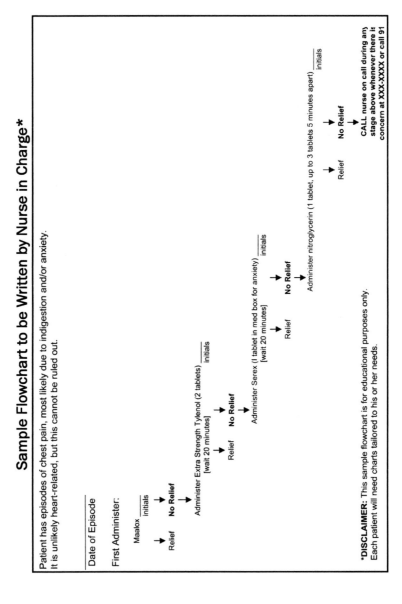

Sample Flowchart to be Written by Nurse in Charge*

Patient has episodes of chest pain, most likely due to indigestion and/or anxiety. It is unlikely heart-related, but this cannot be ruled out.

Date of Episode _____

First Administer:

Maalox _____
    initials

Relief   **No Relief**

Administer Extra Strength Tylenol (2 tablets) _____
[wait 20 minutes]   initials

Relief   **No Relief**

Administer Serex (1 tablet in med box for anxiety) _____
[wait 20 minutes]   initials

Relief   **No Relief**

Administer nitroglycerin (1 tablet, up to 3 tablets 5 minutes apart) _____
    initials

Relief   **No Relief**

CALL nurse on call during any stage above whenever there is concern at XXX-XXXX or call 91

***DISCLAIMER:** This sample flowchart is for educational purposes only. Each patient will need charts tailored to his or her needs.*

217

Sample Morning Schedule

A.M. shift 8:00 AM-12:00 noon	Date	Date	Date	Date	Date
	Initials	Initials	Initials	Initials	Initials
Assist with bathing (shower, bath, or sponge bath)					
Apply lotion after bath					
Skin care: Note any redness or open areas					
Assist with dressing					
Cue before-breakfast meds					
Prepare breakfast and assist as needed					
Cue breakfast and after-breakfast meds					
Offer fluids throughout the shift					
Do laundry as needed					
Prepare lunch and assist as needed					
Offer to assist with toileting before leaving					
Be sure patient has Lifeline					
Leave a drink and snacks at the bedside before leaving					
Keep track of BM and document on BM log					
Make entries in log book and flow sheet and note in log book if skin is red					
If skin has broken down, call supervising nurse or hospice nurse					

Sample Evening Schedule

Evening shift 5:00 pm-9:00 pm	Date	Date	Date	Date	Date
	Initials	Initials	Initials	Initials	Initials
Prepare supper and assist as needed					
Cue medications					
Shop at grocery, pharmacy, etc. as needed					
Skin care: note if any redness or open areas					
Help prepare for bed/ nighttime routine					
Offer fluids and leave a snack at the bedside before leaving patient					
Put home-delivered meals in the fridge after using what is needed for supper					
Manage the food in the fridge — date food, throw out spoiled or out-of-date food					
Document in the flow sheet, log book, and bowel movement log					
Be sure patient has Lifeline					
Laundry as needed					

Sample Night Schedule

Night shift 11:00 pm-7:00 am	Date	Date	Date	Date	Date
	Initials	Initials	Initials	Initials	Initials
Help patient to the bathroom as needed					
Comfort care					
Be sure patient has Lifeline					
Laundry as needed					
Document in the flow sheet, log book, and bowel movement log					

Sample Information Management Sheet

Name	Address	Phone #	E-mail
Family/relatives			
Aunt Ginny			
Cousin Frank			
Your parent's friends			
Neighbors			
Doctor/specialty			
Dr. Smith/*Primary Care*			
/Internist			
/Ophthalmologist			
/Neurologist			
/Audiologist			
/Gastroenterologist			
/Hematologist			
/Cardiologist			
/Dermatologist			
Your parent's lawyer(s)			
Your parent's financial advisor			
Church/synagogue			
Pastor/Rabbi			
Congregation members			

Name	Address	Phone #	E-mail
Service Providers			
Repairmen			
Electrician			
Plumber			
Lawn Service			
Snow removal			
General contractor			
Roofer			
Trash collector			
In-home care			
Main contact person			
Names of aides			
In-home hospice			
Main contact person			
Residential hospice			
Main contact person			
Nurses			
CNAs			
Hospital			
Rehab facility			
Local bank			
Local pharmacy			

Sample Medical Appointments Log

Your Parent's Medicare and/or Medicaid #(s)_____and Insurance Card #_____

Doctor/specialty	Phone #	Date of appt.	Outcome/ recommendations	New prescription(s)	Follow-up appt
Dr. Jones Gastroenterologist		1/22 2:30	Endoscopy Referred to clinic	Nexium®	1 week after procedure
Dr. Smith Cardiologist		2/3 9:00	Echocardiogram		1 month
Dr. Black Dermatologist		2/10 11:00	Biopsy	Apply Neosporin®	1 week

Sample Prescription Medications Log

Your Parent's Medicare and/or Medicaid #(s)_____ and Insurance Card #_____

Brand name	Generic	Condition	Dose*	Refill date	Prescribing MD
Lipitor®**	atorvastatin	Hyperlipidemia (high cholesterol)	40 mg/once a day		Cardiologist
Lasix®**	furosemide	Edema/congestive heart failure	40 mg/ twice a day		Primary care MD
Toprol-XL®	metoprolol	Hypertension (high blood pressure)	50 mg/once a day		Primary care MD
Advil®	ibuprofen	Arthritis	400 mg/up to four times a day		Primary care MD
Nitrostat®	nitroglycerin	Angina pectoris	0.03 mg/ every 5 minutes up to 3 tablets		Cardiologist

*Doses are examples only and are within recommended dosing according to product package inserts.

**Examples of side effects:

Lipitor — common side effects include headache, constipation, diarrhea, gas, upset stomach, stomach pain, rash and muscle and joint pain. See product insert for more information: http://www.drugs.com/lipitor.html

Lasix — the most common side effect is frequent urination, followed by muscle cramps, weakness, dizziness, confusion, thirst, upset stomach, vomiting, blurred vision, headache, restlessness, constipation. See product insert for more information: http://www.drugs.com/lasix.html

Most elders take more than five prescription medications a day, and some take as many as 12! Therefore, it is vitally important that you and the caregivers are aware of the potential side effects of every drug, as well as the possible side effects from drug-drug interactions. And it is extremely important that all involved physicians know exactly which medications your parent is taking. Lasix, for example, is incompatible with many other prescribed drugs. For people taking Lasix, it is important to replenish electrolytes (potassium, in particular) that are lost because of frequent urination. Foods rich in potassium are bananas, prunes, raisins, and orange juice. If need be, a potassium supplement can be taken. Patients taking Lasix should have routinely scheduled blood work.

As mentioned earlier, researchers at Yale University School of Medicine found that more than 90% of seniors taking five or more medications experience one or more "mildly bothersome" side effects, such as changes in mood, insomnia, impaired balance, fatigue, and/or dizziness. One third of the study participants attributed these changes to one of their medications.[10]

> DISCLAIMER: The sample prescription medication log
> is NOT a real example. It is for educational purposes
> only.

Note: You may want your parent to have copies of these logs as well. If you can print them so that they fit in a wallet, that might help. Or keep them posted on the side of the refrigerator. This way, if your parent is whisked away by ambulance, the paramedics may see the log, as they may also be looking for the DNR normally posted on the refrigerator.

Note: The importance of identifying prescriptions by their brand and generic names is to prevent accidental double dosing.

Appendix C

Annotated List of Web Sites

Finding care

- **Eldercare Locator.** Helps you find state and local ombudsmen and agencies serving the elderly. http://www.eldercare.gov/Eldercare/Public/Home.asp

- **Assisted Living Federation of America.** Offers a wide range of resources, including a database of assisted living facilities searchable by location or parent company. http://www.alfa.org/i4a/pages/index.cfm?pageid=3278

- **CareScout.** If you need assistance in finding advocacy and other services for your elderly parents, and if your parents are able to pay their own way, this is a good resource. They charge $499 for their services. http://web.carescout.com/carescoutsite/

- **Getcare.com.** Provides a user-friendly tool to help you fill out a needs assessment. They also list a variety of services, including daycare for patients with Alzheimer's, respite for caregivers, transportation services, financial services, geriatric management, grief support, and a host of other services. You can search by state and county. http://www.getcare.com

- **National Association of Professional Geriatric Care Managers.** Search for a geriatric care manager by location. http://www.caremanager.org

- **SNAPforSeniors.** Offers a searchable housing locator with 60,000 listings, including facilities for assisted living, residential care, nursing care and rehabilitation, continuing care retirement, and independent living. http://www.snapforseniors.com/default.aspx?affiliateid=107954

- **SeniorLIvingGuide.com.** Dedicated to the Carolinas, Virginia, and Florida. Within these states you can search by region for all types of senior housing, case managers, lawyers, and more. Includes a glossary of industry jargon. http://www.seniorlivingguide.com

- **UComparehealth care.** Provides various search engines to find physicians, nursing homes, hospitals, mammography centers, etc. Included are data on quality, staffing, and outcomes from government sources. http://www.ucomparehealth care.com

- **Family Caregiving 101.** A separate "how-to" site by the National Family Caregivers Association (NFCA), with advice on time management, asking for help, navigating the health care maze, and communicating with insurance companies and hospitals. http:// www.familycaregiving101.org/top_10/

- **Family Caregiver Alliance.** Offers tips on a wide range of topics, including how to hire help, assess needs, determine if your parent should move into an alternative facility or in with you, and more. http:// www.caregiver.org/caregiver/jsp/home.jsp

- **MIT's AgeLab.** Devoted to creating new innovations that include driving and personal mobility, independent living and caregiving, retirement and longevity, and much more. Learn the latest inventions and innovations that will help your parent live longer, safely and more independently and will help you, the caregiver. There are constant new listings on this site, and their work is very exciting. http://web.mit.edu/agelab

- **National Alliance for Caregiving.** Offers ways to find assistance, answers to a host of questions, and helpful advice for you and your loved one. Reviews more than 1,000 books, videos, Web sites, and links. http://www.caregiving.org

- **National Family Caregivers Association.** Provides statistics, research and policy reports,

tip sheets, first-person accounts, a newsletter, and an exhaustive resource list.
http://www.nfcacares.org

- **The New Old Age Blog.** Articles are written by Jane Gross from the New York Times and cover a broad range of topics, such as why hire a geriatric care manager, learning to prevent falls, how to choose long-term care, and a host of other subjects. Caregivers of elderly parents can ask all sorts of questions on her blog. She truly offers a wealth of information.
http://newoldage.blogs.nytimes.com/author/jane-gross

- **Caring Connections.** This is a national consumer and community engagement initiative to improve care at the end of life — it is a program of the National Hospice and Palliative Care Organization (NHPCO) and is supported by a grant from The Robert Wood Johnson Foundation. You will find links for state-by-state advance directives and for finding hospice in your area.
http://www.caringinfo.org

- **Caring.com.** Blogs, discussions, and to-do lists as well as advice on caregiving, long-term care, talking with elders, and insurance issues.
http://www.caring.com

- **Eldercare Online.** Provides a wealth of information covering a broad range of topics. http://www.ec-online.net

- **Attentive Care.** Specializes in live-in companionship for the elderly. http://www.attentivehome health care.com

- **Medicare and Medicaid.** Offer two in-home programs for the frail elderly. Check your state for details. http://www.medicare.gov/nursing/alternatives/SHMO.asp and http://www.cms.hhs.gov/pace/lppo/list.asp

How to pay for care

- **Govbenefits.gov.** Find out if your parent is eligible for benefits provided by a variety of government programs. http://www.govbenefits.gov/govbenefits_en.portal

- **Medicare.gov.** How to plan and pay for long-term care and how to choose among drug plans. Research the inspection findings of all the nation's skilled nursing facilities. http://www.medicare.gov

- **National Institute on Aging.** Discover ongoing research on aging and find clinical trials seeking participants. http://www.nia.nih.gov

- **U.S. Administration on Aging.** Find brief fact sheets on aging and links to outside resources for an assortment of caregiving issues, including financial planning, residential options, in-home services, case management, and the law. http://www.aoa.dhhs.gov/eldfam/eldfam.aspx

- **BenefitsCheckUp.** A search tool developed by the National Council on Aging to determine eligibility for 1,300 benefit programs that help pay for medications, health care, utilities, and so forth. http://www.strengthforcaring.com/manual/index.html

- **National Center for Home Equity Conversion.** A consumer's guide to reverse mortgages from a nonprofit with no ties to the industry. Includes frequently asked questions. http://www.reverse.org/Basic%20Q&A.HTM

- **ReverseMortgage.org.** Provides a calculator and search tool to find local lenders, with links to their Web sites. http://www.reversemortgage.org

- **Reverse Mortgage.** Learn the ins and outs of reverse mortgages, and understand their limitations and shortcomings as well as their promises. http://www.fool.com/personal-finance/retirement/2008/05/19/your-house-can-pay-you-to-retire.aspx?terms=reverse+mortgage&vstest=search_042607_linkdefault

- **Elderweb.** Covers a broad range of topics from aging, diseases, and elder law to Medicare, Medicaid, and more. http://www.elderweb.com/home/

- **National Care Planning Council.** Offers articles and links on a wide range of topics such as elder law, hospice care, reverse mortgages, funeral and burial plans, etc. http://www.longtermcarelink.net

- **Care.com.** Provides a state-by-state directory that lists data related to seven areas of senior services, including financial planning and transportation. http://www.care.com

End-of-life issues

- **American Bar Association Aging Tool Kit.** Offers a 10-step process for making end-of-life decisions with worksheets, suggestions, and links. http://www.abanet.org/aging/toolkit

- **National Association for Home Care and Hospice.** The National Association for Home Care and Hospice is the nation's largest trade association representing the interests and concerns of home care agencies, hospices, and home care aide organizations. The Home Care/ Hospice Agency Locator contains the most comprehensive database of more than 20,000 home care and hospice agencies. Use this resource to find all the agencies in any particular area of the country. http://www.nahc.org

- **National Cancer Institute (NCI). Advanced Cancer: Living Each Day and Cancer Facts: End-of-Life Care: Questions and Answers.** Offer very good suggestions on how caregivers can provide emotional support and physical comfort. Also lists the signs that death is near and offers suggestions for what the caregiver can do to keep the patient comfortable. http://www.cancer.gov/cancertopics/advancedcancer

- **The National Hospice and Palliative Care Organization.** An excellent search tool for finding a hospice, as well as guides on issues related to palliative care, including Medicare coverage and techniques for communicating end-of-life wishes. Also provides a state-by-state link to download your state's advance directives. http://www.nhpco.org/templates/1/homepage.cfm

- **Hospice Foundation of America.** Information on end-of-life issues such as pain management. Provides several blogs as well as a list of FAQs. Personal stories about death and dying can also be found on the site. In a section called "Caregivers Corner," you will find links to reading lists and a self-assessment tool for caregivers to analyze their own strengths and

weaknesses.
http://www.hospicefoundation.org

- **Hospice Net. Preparing for Approaching Death**. Provides detailed information about what to expect before someone dies, the changes to look for, and ways to comfort them emotionally and physically. http://www.hospicenet.org/html/preparing_for.html

- **National Care Planning Council**. Offers articles and links on a wide range of topics including elder law, hospice care, reverse mortgages, funeral and burial plans, etc. http://www.longtermcarelink.net

Note: Information about hospice is available from your local hospital, your state hospice organizations, or the National Hospice Helpline (800-658-8898) as well as from the National Council of Hospice Professionals Physician Section. You can also find information about hospice from the American Cancer Society, the American Association of Retired Persons (AARP), and the Social Security Administration.

Legal

- **U.S. Administration on Aging**. Find brief fact sheets on aging and links to outside resources for an assortment of caregiving issues, including financial planning, residential options, in-home

services, case management, and the law. http://
www.aoa.dhhs.gov/eldfam/eldfam.aspx

- **MetLife Mature Market Institute**. Provides
many reports from a research arm of the
insurance company that include advice on
communicating with health care professionals,
legal matters, and offers. Also offers a
newsletter that provides stats, trends, and
information on issues related to aging,
including retirement planning and financing,
workforce demographics, international aging,
caregiving, long-term care, health, and retiree
benefits from a variety of sources.
http://www.metlife.com/Applications/
Corporate/WPS/CDA/PageGenerator/
0,2752,P2801,00.html

- **American Bar Association Aging Tool Kit**.
Offers a 10-step process for making end-of-life
decisions with worksheets, suggestions, and
links. http://www.abanet.org/aging/toolkit/

- **BenefitsCheckUp**. A search tool developed by
the National Council on Aging to determine
eligibility for 1,300 benefit programs that help
pay for medications, health care, utilities, and so
forth. http://www.strengthforcaring.com/
manual/index.html

- **National Academy of Elder Law Attorneys**.
Educates lawyers about the needs of the elderly

and allows you to search for a lawyer in your area who is a member of the association. Provides questions and answers that serve as a guide when hiring a lawyer who specializes in elder law. http://www.naela.com

- **Nolo**. Do-it-yourself legal advice for nominal fees. An interactive online service for wills, powers of attorney, and other documents. http://www.nolo.com

- **Senior Law Home Page**. Find information on elder law, Medicare, Medicaid, Medicaid planning, guardianship, estate planning, trusts, and the rights of the elderly and disabled. Provides information for families and advocates as well as lawyers. http://www.seniorlaw.com

- **U.S. Living Will Registry®**. The U.S. Living Will Registry electronically stores advance directives and makes them available to health care providers 24 hours a day via secure Internet, telephone, or fax. Many health care providers and community partners provide the registry's service at a discounted rate or even free of charge. You can find a participating member in your state. http://www.uslivingwillregistry.com

- **The National Hospice and Palliative Care Organization**. An excellent search tool for finding a hospice as well as guides on issues related to palliative care, including Medicare coverage and techniques for communicating end-of-life wishes. Also provides a state-by-state link to download your state's advance directives. http://www.nhpco.org/templates/1/homepage.cfm

- **National Care Planning Council.** Offers articles and links on a wide range of topics such as elder law, hospice care, reverse mortgages, funeral and burial plans, etc. http://www.longtermcarelink.net

- **Caring Connections.** Provides free advance directives for each state. http://www.caringinfo.org/stateaddownload

Advocacy

- **AARP.** Provides a wealth of information on a vast array of topics including political position papers, member discounts, demographic research, online versions of its bulletin, and magazine and consumer advice. http://www.aarp.org

- **Center for Medicare Advocacy.** Detailed information about what Medicare covers, how to enroll, and, if necessary, appeal denial of claims. http://www.medicareadvocacy.org

- **Medicare Rights Center.** Advice on how to work the system. How to appeal private drug plans, the latest changes in Medicare, everything you need to know about Medicare's drug benefit, and a hotline for questions and complaints. http://www.medicarerights.org

- **National Association of Area Agencies on Aging (AAA).** A network of local Area Agency on Aging and Title VI programs that provides answers to questions about home and community-based services for older adults and family caregivers. Also includes articles on caregiving, policy reports, and links to eldercare service agencies. http://www.n4a.org

- **Ombudsmen.** Can serve as advocates for those in nursing homes. http://www.ltcombudsman.org/static_pages/ombudsmen.cfm

Help for caregivers

- **Strength for Caring.** A compendium of articles that cover topics such as balancing work and family, stress relief, food, fitness and wellness, grief, death and dying, and much more. http://www.strengthforcaring.com/manual/index.html

- **Third Age.** Articles, questions, and answers from the experts, checklists for caregivers, and suggestions for caring for loved ones with Alzheimer's. http://www.thirdage.com/caregiving

- **Children of Aging Parents**. Support groups, both online and face-to-face. A caregiver guide offers helpful hints, and a very extensive list of links is provided that should prove quite useful. http://www.caps4caregivers.org

- **CareGiverHelper.** A site to assist and provide support to family members who are taking care of an aging parent. http://www.caregiverhelper.com

- **Eldercare Online**. Provides a wealth of information covering a broad range of topics. http://www.ec-online.net

Needs assessment tools

- **Getcare.com**. Provides a user-friendly tool to help you fill out a needs assessment. A variety of services are also listed, including day care for patients with Alzheimer's, respite for caregivers, transportation services, financial services, geriatric management, grief support, and a host of other services. You can search by state and county. http://www.getcare.com

- **How to Talk About Driving**. The Hartford Financial Services Group, Inc. and MIT's AgeLab have conducted original research that expands the understanding of older drivers and their families as they deal with changes in driving abilities. Together they have developed guidelines to help families initiate productive and caring conversations with older adults about driving safety. http://www.thehartford.com/talkwitholderdrivers/

Housing and services

- **Fall Prevention Center of Excellence**. Advice on home renovation and remodeling that makes performing tasks easier, reduces accidents, and supports independent living. http://www.homemods.org

- **National Center for Assisted Living**. Provides a national clearinghouse of information. A user-friendly "facility finder" factors in cost, method of payment, mobility, dietary needs, activities, and amenities. http://www.ncal.org

- **Granny Flats and Elder Cottages**. Temporary modular housing designed with the needs of seniors can be installed on the property of a family member or friend. Before buying or leasing a unit, check zoning codes. http://seniorlving.about.com/od/housingoptions/a/echo/html

Ancillary health care service providers

- **Visiting Nurse Associations of America**. Provides a search engine to search for home health services nationwide. Includes frequently asked questions and provides a list of questions

to ask service providers. http://
www.vnaa.org/vnaa/gen/html~home.aspx

- **National Association of Senior Move Managers.** A not-for-profit, professional association dedicated to assisting older adults with the physical and emotional demands of downsizing, relocating, or modifying their homes. Provides a list of senior move managers. http://www.nasmm.org

High-tech devices for today and tomorrow

- **Passive monitoring devices.** Passive monitoring systems allow aging seniors to stay in their homes longer and grow old with dignity. A variety of monitoring options are available and include the installation of motion sensors and a remote monitoring system that sends data to the caregiver and to the provider of the system.
  QuietCare: http://www.quietcare.com
  SimplyHome: http://www.simplyhome-cmi.com
  GrandCare: http://www.grandcare.com
  Healthsense: http://www.healthsense.com

- **MIT's AgeLab.** Researchers at MIT are striving to find ways to empower individuals and their caregivers with the knowledge and skills to make better health decisions and to design tools that will assist in the management of chronic diseases. Their research includes improving driving and personal mobility, independent living and caregiving, retirement and longevity, and much more. Learn about the latest inventions and innovations that will help your parent live safely and independently and that will also help you, the caregiver. There are constant new listings on this site, and their work is very exciting. http://web.mit.edu/agelab

- **Prodigy Voice**. Talking glucose meter designed for the blind or visually impaired individual with diabetes. http://www.prlog.org/ 10056454-prodigy-voice-talking-glucose-meter-for-blind-now-available-from-western-diabetic-supplies.htm

- **Autominder**. A cognitive orthotic that provides users with reminders about their daily activities. Unlike simpler systems that just sound an alarm, Autominder is smart enough to make adjustments based on a client's behavior. For example, if the elder needs to be reminded to use the bathroom every three hours but they go on their own within the 3-hour window, Autominder automatically makes the adjustment and restarts the 3-hour clock. For some, Autominder could be used as an adjunct to in-home care; for others, it could be the first step before in-home care is introduced. It has great potential in helping elderly with cognitive deficiencies to remain in their homes longer.

[Autominder: An Intelligent Cognitive Orthotic System for people with Memory Impairment. Pollack ME, Brown L, Colbry D, McCarthy E, Orosz C, et al.] http://www.eecs.umich.edu/~sailesh/ras03.pdf

- **Center for Aging Services Technologies (CAST).** Leading the charge to expedite the development, evaluation, and adoption of emerging technologies that can improve the aging experience. CAST has become an international coalition of more than 400 technology companies, aging services organizations, research universities, and government representatives. Provides many links to news about exciting technologies that are in the pipeline. http://www.agingtech.org/newsroom/newsroom.aspx

- **iShoe**. Currently being tested in about 60 people and awaiting patent approval. It contains sensors that determine how well a person is balancing. The main objective is to gather data and to get the person to a doctor before they have a fall. http://www.msnbc.msn.com/id/25949023

- **Smart Technology for Aging, Disability and Independence: The State of the Science.** Brings together current research and technological developments from engineering, computer science, and the rehabilitation sciences and details how its applications can promote continuing independence for older persons and those with disabilities. By William C. Mann, John Wiley and Sons, Inc. 2005. http://www.wiley.com/WileyCDA/WileyTitle/productCd-0471696943.html

- **The LifeShirt® System.** A noninvasive ambulatory monitoring system that continuously collects, records and analyzes a broad range of cardiopulmonary parameters for viewing in real-time or for postanalysis. Embedded with sensors, it is worn as a lightweight undershirt. In addition to collecting cardiopulmonary data, it also can monitor EEG/EOG, periodic leg movement, temperature, end tidal CO_2, blood oxygen saturation, blood pressure, and cough. http://www.vivometrics.com/research/clinical_trials/view_our_products/product_line.php

- **ClarityLife C900™.** This mobile phone is twice as loud as other cell phones and has large buttons for ease of use. Users can get help quickly by pressing the large red emergency button. The phone calls and sends text messages to five preprogrammed numbers, such as those of family, friends, neighbors, or emergency personnel. It cycles through the five contacts until someone picks up. To order, visit

http://www.clarityproducts.com/products/
listing/item3289.asp

- **Ceiva Digital Photo Frame**. Can reduce
  isolation, loneliness, and depression. Help your
  parent stay connected with family, friends,
  grandchildren, and their activities and share
  photos from your family vacations. This device
  can be preloaded with up to 70 digital photos or
  be plugged into a home phone line to receive
  transmitted photos. Using the phone line (an
  optional feature at additional cost), the frame
  silently dials a local number each night to
  receive new photos e-mailed to the frame,
  without interruption to phone service or
  charges to the phone line. To order, visit http://
  www.ceiva.com/cstore/ct/cstore_catalog.jsp

Medications, herbs, and supplements

- **Drugs.com** is a great resource for finding out
  which medications do not mix well with others.
  It provides a wealth of information on 24,000
  prescription medications, over-the-counter
  medications, and natural products. It also
  covers a number of topics including FDA alerts
  and clinical trial results. The site is very user-
  friendly. http://www.drugs.com

- **Entrez Pub Med** is a government site primarily
  for medical professionals. It provides many
  thousands of medical articles with abstracts on a

very wide range of topics. You can search by author, title of article, illness, medicines or supplements, and herbs. It has articles predominantly on medical research and medicine, but you can find a few articles on herbs and supplements. http://www.ncbi.nlm.nih.gov/pubmed and http://www.nlm.nih.gov/medicineplus/druginformation.html

- **Supplements that help people with Alzheimer's**. To find out what kind of lifestyle changes and supplements can help patients with Alzheimer's, visit http://health.nytimes.com/health/guides/disease/alzheimers-disease/overview

- **Prescribing narcotics**. "Physicians need to know that if these medications are used properly, prescribing them is as routine as prescribing a blood pressure medicine. It doesn't need to carry any more of a stigma." http://www.jhu.edu/~jhumag/0699web/pain.html

How to prevent falls

- **For more information about learning how to prevent falls**, go to http://newoldage.nytimes.com. Jane Gross lists links to a video called "The Good News on Fall Prevention", a list of medications that can increase the risk of falls, and much more.

- **The NoFalls exercise program manual**, which was developed for trained professionals, is available free of charge in electronic format at http://www.monash.edu.au/muarc//projects/nofalls/

- **The Centers for Disease Control and Prevention (CDC)** developed the **Compendium of Effective Community-Based Interventions** that provides specific interventions to help reduce falls among seniors. The interventions include tai chi and other exercise classes combined with a daily exercise program done at home. All of their materials are free. http://www.cdc.gov/ncipc/preventingfalls/CDCCompendium_030508.pdf

- The **CDC** also provides brochures on **fall prevention**. These brochures are free of charge. http://www.cdc.gov/homeandrectional safety.falls/index-pr.html

- The **CDC** provides a **Home Fall Prevention Checklist** for older adults. The checklist helps address hazards in the home that could cause an older adult to fall. http://www.cdc.gov/ncipc/pub-res/toolkit/Falls_ToolKit/DesktopPDF/English/ booklet_Eng_desktop.pdf

Nursing homes — ratings and locators

- **HealthGrades**. Comparisons and 1- to 5-star ranking of nursing homes. The first report is $9.95, and each additional one is $2.95. http://www.healthgrades.com

- **UComparehealth care**. Provides various search engines to find physicians, nursing homes, hospitals, mammography centers, etc. Included are data on quality, staffing, and outcomes from government sources. http://www.ucomparehealth care.com

- **National Watch List of nursing homes**. If you find that a nursing home is your only option, MemberoftheFamily.net provides free reports based on government findings of 16,000 nursing homes. This site includes a National Watch List that lists nursing homes cited for numerous violations or those that have had numerous, substantiated complaints. http://www.MemberoftheFamily.net

- **State and Federal Assessment of nursing homes**. Each agency issues a report on any deficiencies it finds at the facility. These reports are collected by the federal government. A summary and comparison of the findings can be accessed at http://www.medicare.gov/ NHcompare

- **The National Citizen's Coalition for Nursing Home Reform**, at http://www.nccnhr.org, offers a consumer guide to choosing a nursing home.

Government (miscellaneous)

- **National Association for Home Care and Hospice (NAHC) Regulatory Affairs Division.** The regulatory staff is often the first to learn of regulatory changes that have both direct and indirect effects on the home health and hospice industry. This up-to-the-minute tracking of key regulatory events enables members to stay ahead of the curve in a rapidly changing health care environment. http://www.nahc.org/regulatory/home.html

- **NIHSeniorHealth.** Look up information on diseases and disorders of old age. This is an authoritative source provided by the National Institutes of Health in collaboration with the National Library of Medicine. The site is very user-friendly and provides large-type and audio versions. http://nihseniorhealth.gov

Recommended Reading

The Art of Dying: How to Leave This World With Dignity and Grace, at Peace With Yourself and Your Loved Ones
Patricia Weenolsen and Bernie S. Siegel
St Martins Press (June 1996)

Chasing Daylight
Eugene O'Kelly
McGraw-Hill; 1st edition (September 24, 2007)

Final Gifts: Understanding the Special Awareness, Needs, and Communications of the Dying
Maggie Callanan and Patricia Kelley
Bantam (February 3, 1997)

Life After Death: The Burden of Proof
Deepak Chopra
Three Rivers Press; Reprint edition (September 16, 2008)

Life after Life: The Investigation of a Phenomenon — Survival of Bodily Death
Raymond Moody. Foreword by Elisabeth Kübler-Ross
HarperOne (March 6, 2001)

The Light Beyond
Raymond Moody
Bantam (August 1, 1989)

Meditation for Beginners
Jack Kornfield
Sounds True, Incorporated; Pap/Com edition (August 1, 2008)

The Mindful Way Through Depression: Freeing Yourself From Chronic Unhappiness
Mark G. Williams, John D. Teasdale, Zindel V. Segal, Jon Kabat-Zinn
The Guilford Press (June 1, 2007)

Mindfulness for Beginners (Audio CD)
Jon Kabat-Zinn
Sounds True Incorporated; Unabridged edition (July 2006)

My Mother: Your Mother: Embracing Slow Medicine, the Compassionate Approach to Caring for Your Aging Loved Ones
Dennis McCullough
Harper 1st edition (February 5, 2008)

On Life After Death
Elisabeth Kübler-Ross, with, foreword by Carolyn Myss
Celestial Arts, Second edition (March 2008)

The One Earth Herbal Sourcebook: Everything You Need to Know About Chinese, Western, and Ayurvedic Herbal Treatments
Alan Keith Tillotson, Nai-shing Hu Tillotson, Robert Abel Jr.
Twin Streams, Kensington Publishing Corp. 2001

Questions On Death and Dying
Elisabeth Kübler-Ross
Scribner; 1st edition (June 9, 1997)

Talking About Death Won't Kill You
Virginia Moore
Workman Publishing Company; 1st edition (September 10, 2001)

Tibetan Book of Living and Dying
Sogyal Rinpoche, Patrick D. Gaffney, Andrew Harvey
HarperOne (March 17, 1994)

Tibetan Book of the Dead
Graham Coleman, Thupten Jinpa, Gyurme Dorje
Penguin Classics; Deluxe edition (January 30, 2007)

Tuesdays With Morrie
Mitch Albom
Time Warner Paperbacks (July 24, 2003)

Unstuck: Your Guide to the Seven-Stage Journey Out of Depression
James S. Gordon
The Penguin Press (June 12, 2008)

References

1. Prince Market Research. Aging in Place in America. Available at: http://www.marketingcharts.com/seniors-fear-loss-of-independence-nursing-homes-more-than-death-034454/ Accessed November 15, 2008. Research was conducted by Prince Market Research and was commissioned by a partnership of Clarity and The EAR Foundation to better understand the health and lifestyle needs of America's aging population. Over 800 seniors and baby boomers were polled.

2. Robert Wood Johnson Foundation. *Advanced Practice Nursing, Pioneering Practices in Palliative Care, Promoting Excellence in End-of-Life Care.* A National Program Office of The Robert Wood Johnson Foundation, 1000 East Beckwith Avenue, Missoula, MT 59812, p 3.

3. Dobkin L. Family friendly burbs turn senior friendly. *Kiplinger Washington Editors, Inc.* April 5, 2008.

4. National Osteoporosis Foundation, Fast Facts on Osteoporosis. Available at: http://www.nof.org/osteoporosis/disease-facts.htm. Accessed November 19, 2008.

5. Shulman M. For better balance, Pilates and tai chi beat yoga. *US News and World Report.* August 7, 2008.

6. Gross J. For the elderly, being heard about life's end. *New York Times.* May 5, 2008. Available at: http://www.nytimes.com/2008/05/05/health/05slow.html. Accessed May 5, 2008.

7. Choi JH, Moon JS, Song R. Effects of Sun-style tai chi exercise on physical fitness and fall prevention in fall- prone older adults. *J Adv Nurs.* 2005;51(2):150-157.

8. The Harvard Medical School, Family Health Guide. Vitamin D recommendations. February 2004. Available at: http:// health.harvard.edu/fhg/updates/update0204a.shtml. Accessed October 15, 2008.

9. http://www.laughternetwork.co.uk/laughter.html. Accessed November 19, 2008.

10. Mozes A. Electronic pillbox helps seniors stick to drug regimens. Healthday, News for Healthier Living. Available at: http://healthday.com. Accessed October 6, 2008.

11. Becker DJ, Gordon RY, Morris, BP, Yorko J, Gordon YJ, Li M *et al*. Simvastatin vs therapeutic lifestyle changes and supplements: randomized primary prevention trial. *Mayo Clinic Proc.* 2008;83(7): 758-764.

12. Houser AN. Nursing Homes Research Report. AARP Public Policy Institute. October 2007.

13. Hendricks M. "Just give me something for the pain." *Johns Hopkins Magazine.* June 1999. Available at: http://www.jhu.edu/~jhumag/0699web/pain.html. Accessed November 21, 2008.

14. The Gallup Poll. Public Grapples With Legality, Morality of Euthanasia. July 13, 2004. Available at: www.gallup.com. Accessed November 21, 2008.

15. Kübler-Ross K. *Questions on Death and Dying.* New York: Macmillan; 1974:84.

16. RA Burt: The Supreme Court speaks: not assisted suicide but a constitutional right to palliative care. *N Engl J Med* 1997; 337:1234.

Registered Trademarks

ADT® is registered trademark of ADT Services AG.

Advil® (ibuprofen) is a registered trademark of Wyeth Consumer health care.

Ativan® (lorazepam) is a registered trademark of Biovail Pharmaceuticals, Inc.

Bach® Flowers is a registered trademark of Bach Flowers Limited.

Compazine® (prochiorperazine) is a registered trademark of Evoke Pharma, Inc.

Depend® is a registered trademark of Kimberly-Clark Corporation.

Dilaudid® (hydromorphone hydrochloride) is a registered trademark of Abbott Laboratories.

Duragesic® (fentanyl transdermal system) CII is a registered trademark of Johnson & Johnson Corporation.

DuoDERM® is a registered trademark of The Purdue Frederick Company.

FallSaver® is a registered trademark of NOCwatch International, Inc.

Feldenkrais® is a registered service mark.

Guido® the Smart Walker is a registered trademark of Haptica.

GrandCare® is a registered trademark of Interages Corporation.

Haldol® (haloperidol) is a registered trademark of Ortho-McNeil Pharmaceutical, Inc.

Healthsense® is a registered trademark of Red Wing Technologies, Inc.

Intel® is a registered trademark of Intel Corporation.

Lasix® (furosemide) is a registered trademark of Sanofi Aventis.

Lifeline® is a registered trademark of Philips Electronics North America Corporation.

LifeShirt® is a registered trademark of VivoMetrics®, Inc.

Lipitor® (atorvastatin) is a registered trademark of Pfizer, Inc.

Maalox® is a registered trademark of Novortis Consumer Health Inc.

MALEM© Enuresis Wireless Remote Bed Alarm is manufactured by Malem Medical.

MedSignals® is a registered trademark of Brue, Vesta L, individual.

Megace® (megestrol) is a registered trademark of Bristol Meyers Squibb.

Metamucil® is a registered trademark of Proctor and Gamble.

MiraLax® (polyethylene glycol 3350) is a registered trademark of Schering-Plough health care Products, Inc.

Neosporin® is a registered trademark of Pfizer, Inc.

Nexium® (esomeprazole) is a registered trademark of AstraZeneca.

Nitrostat® (nitroglycerin) is a registered trademark of Park, Davis and Company.

Prevacid® (lansoprazole) is a registered trademark of Tap Pharmaceutical Products, Inc.

Prodigy® Voice is a registered trademark of Diagnostic Devices, Inc.

QuietCare® is a registered trademark of Living Independently Group, Inc.

Rescue Remedy® is a registered trademark of Bach Flowers Limited.

Rituxan® (rituximab) is a registered trademark of Genentech, Inc.

SimplyHome™ is a registered trademark of Community Management Initiative, Inc.

Talking® Sign is a registered trademark of Talking Signs, Inc.

Toprol-XL® (metoprolol succinate) is a registered trademark of AstraZeneca Pharmaceuticals.

Tylenol® (acetaminophen) is a registered trademark of Johnson and Johnson Corporation.

Zocor® (simvastatin) is a registered trademark of Merck & Co., Inc.

Index

senior center 31, 41, 49, 76, 156
seniors 1, 3, 9, 13, 19, 25, 27–28, 33, 38–39, 41, 44, 54, 57, 60–61, 65–68, 71, 81, 84, 86–88, 90, 148, 157–158, 163, 225, 228, 241–242, 248
sensors 57–61, 63–64, 67–68, 97, 107, 242, 244–245
Shahbaz 86
side effects 24, 38, 54–56, 115–116, 118, 146, 150, 179, 224–225
SimplyHome 59, 242
skin breakdown 119, 152
sleep-wake cycle 48
slow medicine 164, 252
Social Managed Care Plan 89–91
social security taxes 78
social workers 23, 108, 139, 141, 158, 187–189, 196, 202, 215
socializing 40, 49, 194, 210
sodium 37
sound sleep 48
staff 4, 65, 74, 86–87, 95, 103–105, 110, 112, 114, 117–118, 120, 122–126, 128, 133–135, 139, 153, 156, 163, 182, 190–191, 194, 199, 202, 205, 210, 214
  bonded 74, 139, 183, 206
  shortage 5, 98, 112–113, 119–120
  staffing ratios 110, 188–190, 203, 216
  turnover 110
stair-climbing wheelchair 21
stamina 41–42, 44
status 23, 103, 106, 117, 124, 129, 151
  mental 6, 13, 154
  physical 154, 158

strength 17, 41, 43–44, 87, 93, 170
stress (management) 6, 19, 30, 50–52, 103–104, 119, 159, 168, 171, 191, 239
stress buster 51
student interns 20
supplemental insurance 15, 22, 31, 189–190
supplementing CNA care 112
supplements 53–56, 246–247

T

tai chi 25, 43–45, 248
talking about death 34, 161–162, 166, 169, 253
Talking Sign 63
termination clause 73, 184–185, 208
termination policy 73, 76, 208
text message 58, 61, 245
The Ride 160
training 43, 65, 74, 123, 129, 183, 206
trans fats 36–37
transportation costs 193
treatment plan 123–124, 182, 205

U

U.S. Department of Health and Human Services 1
U.S. Department of Housing and Urban Development (HUD) 88
uBox 70
University of Massachusetts Amherst 65, 96
unsteady 21, 23

About the Author

Maria Tadd is a freelance medical writer. Her writing covers a broad spectrum including promotional materials for the pharmaceutical industry and the professional medical community, articles on spirituality and holistic health, haiku poems, a book on elder care, book chapters highlighting the use of supplements to prevent and treat diseases, interviews, and book reviews. A graduate of the New England School of Acupuncture and a life-long student of holistic health, meditation, and nutrition, she has a unique understanding of how to merge Eastern and Western perspectives. Maria's knowledge of medications, herbs, and supplements helped keep her mother healthy for decades until her death at age 95.

LaVergne, TN USA
19 May 2010
183272LV00001B/186/P